# St. George
# and the
# Chinese Dragon

## Lt. Colonel H.B. Vaughan
## 7th Rajputs

*With a Foreword by*
*John Adamson*

THE ALEXIUS PRESS

*A CIP catalogue record for this book is available
from the British Library.*

© *The original text :    Colonel Vaughan's Estate*
© *Editor's Foreword:   John Adamson 2000*

*ISBN: 0 951 9886 4 6*

*Typeset by Beth Emanuel
2 Magnaville Road, Bushey, Herts*

*Printed and bound by The Lowfield Printing Company,
Dartford, Kent.*

*The original text by Lt. Colonel Vaughan was published by
C. Arthur Pearson Ltd., London, in 1902.*

*Published by*

THE ALEXIUS PRESS LIMITED 2000

The cover:
A Bengal Lancer of the 1st (Duke of York's Own)
Regiment (Skinner's Horse)

# CONTENTS

Page

LIST OF ILLUSTRATIONS AND MAPS                    Page

Monochrome illustrations

Colour illustrations

Four pages of colour reproductions of Colonel Vaughan's original water colours appear between pages 80 and 81. These, and the cover illustration, also by Colonel Vaughan, are reproduced by courtesy of Captain Hardie.

Maps

Spelling of names on the maps is in accordance with usage current in 1900, but variant spellings of some names are to be found at that time.

Maps designed by ML Design,
204 Blackfriars Foundry, London SE1

# PREFACE

I came across *St. George and the Chinese Dragon* fortuitously, while searching at the British Library for a book of travel, adventure or military history with a view to possible republication. The title aroused interest; the text turned out to have freshness, directness and brevity, characteristics which were lacking in many of the books I had been reading, which seemed best left in the obscurity of the British Library book stacks.

When I first read *St. George and the Chinese Dragon* I had only a general knowledge of the Boxer Rising and the Relief of the Legations and no knowledge of the life of the author, Colonel (as he became) Vaughan. The book had all the merits of an eye-witness account by a person directly involved in events, but was lacking in context. The reader plunging straight into the action might well feel somewhat disorientated, wondering how such strange events had come about.

The republication of this book, I felt, could be justified only if the reader could be given sufficient background information. This I have attempted to provide in the present volume. The purpose of the Foreword and footnotes is to assist understanding of the text, not to moralise on aspects of Vaughan's account which may strike the reader more strangely now than they would have done some hundred years ago.

As to Vaughan himself, my initial investigations gave no hint of the most adventurous aspects of his past as described in the Foreword. In taking matters further I was greatly assisted by the Vaughan family including Colonel Vaughan's daughter, the late Irene Vaughan, whom I visited at Le Catioroc, the house on the Guernsey coast where Vaughan had spent his last years, and who recalled accounts of her father's adventures in Persia. Among the family records was the document which Vaughan modestly described in his Introduction to *St. George*

1

*and the Chinese Dragon* as a "diary", in reality a remarkable illustrated record of the Relief Expedition, which had been seen and favourably endorsed by Lord Kitchener, Commander-in-Chief in India 1902-09.

In 1999 a new account of the Boxer Rising and the Siege and Relief of the Legations, Diana Preston's *Besieged in Peking*, was published, and included a number of quotations from *St. George and the Chinese Dragon*. Along with the hundredth anniversary of the Siege of the Legations, approaching as this book is being produced, Mrs Preston's recognition of the value of Vaughan's account makes this an opportune time for *St. George and the Chinese Dragon* to be republished.

In addition to acknowledging the help of the Vaughan family, I should like to express my appreciation of the assistance given by the staff of the India Office Library, the London Library, the Public Record Office, the Priaulx Library, Guernsey, the Library and Map Room of the Royal Geographical Society, the Archivists of Charterhouse School and University College London, and by Professor Hugh Baker of the School of Oriental and African Studies, who gave valuable help with the interpretation of the photograph of a Boxer and other matters. Last, but certainly not least, I should like to thank my Alexius Press colleagues Michael Turner, particularly for his research which helped me find the Vaughan family, and Len Hudson, for his unfailing help and encouragement during the editorial process. Views expressed in the Foreword are, of course, entirely my own responsibility.

Acknowledgement is made to A.P. Watt Ltd. on behalf of The National Trust for places of Historic Interest or Natural Beauty, for permission to reproduce the extract from *Recessional* which appears in the Foreword.

**John Adamson**
*London June 2000*

2

# Editor's Foreword

*St. George and the Chinese Dragon* starts with a soldier's directness: the author's Indian Army regiment, the 7$^{th}$ Rajputs, is ordered to prepare for service in China. Henry Vaughan explains that most of the British officers were away, but with a modesty not always characteristic of military memoirs, does not bring out the fact that, promoted to the rank of Major only in April 1900, he found himself two months later in command of a regiment on a most exacting, and exciting, expedition.

Colonel Vaughan, as he became, gives no preliminary explanation of why British forces were being sent to China: he goes straight into the action. Those of his contemporaries who purchased his book would have recalled at least the immediate background to the events described. The modern reader, distanced by a century from those events, may well find it helpful to have some information on Chinese history and the circumstances of the Siege of the Foreign Legations and the despatch of the Relief Force.

China is often thought (not least by the Chinese) as having developed, until modern times, very much in isolation from the outside world. However, there are parallels between the early development of the Chinese Empire and the flowering of the classical civilisations of the West. The unification of China under the Ch'in and Han dynasties took place as Rome was expanding its empire around the Mediterranean. Subsequently China and Europe alike fell victim to invasions of nomadic peoples from central Asia. The Roman Empire in the West collapsed, to be replaced in due course by nation states; the Chinese Empire fragmented, but was reunited under the Sui dynasty in A.D. 589, reaching a high point under the T'ang

3

Dynasty (618-907), when Chinese civilisation was far in advance of that in the West.

China and the West again came under a common threat when the Mongols, united under Genghis Khan by 1206, embarked on conquests which exceeded any so far seen in human history. To the west, Mongol armies swept across Russia and won victories in Poland and Hungary – they remained undefeated and might have reached the Atlantic but withdrew following the death of Great Khan Ogedei in 1241. To the east, the northern part of the Chinese Empire was conquered early in the thirteenth century, and the rest (the Sung Empire) in 1279. Mongol ambitions went as far as attempted conquests of Java and Japan.

In effect, China became part of the Mongol Empire, but Mongol imperial rule had some beneficial characteristics. China was united, its influence increased, foreign trade developed, and there was a measure of religious tolerance. However, natural disasters and political mistakes combined to weaken Mongol rule, and secret societies formed – a feature of Chinese history which was to recur, notably, so far as this book is concerned, as a precursor to the Boxer Rising. In the fourteenth century it was the "Red Turbans" who attracted sufficient support to enable their leader, Chu Yuan-chang, to drive the Mongols from Peking and found a new dynasty, the Ming, in 1368.

The West came to have some knowledge of China under Mongol rule through Marco Polo's account of his travels. Questions have been raised about the authenticity of Marco Polo's book, but even if his account cannot necessarily be regarded as all literally true, it did give a good impression, whether based on his own experiences or those of others, of China at the time of Kublai Khan, and aroused much interest. It was not until the Ming Dynasty, however, that the West became significantly involved in the economic, political and religious life of China.

The first European nation to establish a trading base in China was Portugal, which occupied Macao in 1557 having already created a far-flung trading empire. The Portuguese were for a time influential at the Ming court, although they came to be resented and were in due course excluded from the court.

The Ming dynasty was eventually weakened by popular revolt and by pressure from a non-Chinese people based in south-east Manchuria who became known as the Manchus. When the dynasty fell in 1644 the Manchus took over and established a line which survived until the end of imperial rule in 1911. Ming loyalists were gradually overcome – their last redoubt was Taiwan, a curious parallel to the situation in the twentieth century, when Taiwan (Formosa) became a refuge for the Chinese Nationalists when the rest of China came under Communist rule.

It is an interesting reflection, therefore, that the Westerners who had contact with the Manchus in the years to come were dealing with people who were themselves foreign invaders of China although ones who assimilated – it might be said over-assimilated – traditional Chinese ways.

The Manchus, ruling as the Ch'ing Dynasty, brought more than a century of order and prosperity to China. This golden age was inaugurated by the Emperor K'ang-hsi whose reign (1662-1722) had similarities with that of his contemporary Louis XIV of France (reigned 1643-1715). K'ang-hsi was a patron of the arts and sciences and rebuilt Peking, severely damaged during the Manchu invasion. While Louis XIV squandered resources on an ultimately unsuccessful attempt to achieve supremacy in Europe by military means, K'ang-hsi pursued a realistic policy of extending Chinese rule and influence, which continued after his death. By the latter part of the eighteenth century, this policy had not only taken China to broadly her present borders (there was some loss of territory in the nineteenth century to Russia, most significantly in the far north-east, beyond Manchuria) but had led to Korea, Siam (Thailand), Annam (Vietnam) and Burma becoming client states.

In the West, curiosity about, and admiration of, China increased in the eighteenth century. Chinese porcelain had been well known in Europe before then, because it was extensively imported during the Ming dynasty. So strong was the association of China with porcelain that the word "china" entered the language to describe porcelain and similar material – tempting Colonel Vaughan into a punning chapter heading. The enthusiasm of eighteenth century European taste for things Chinese went beyond porcelain however into what was known as "chinoiserie" in decoration and objets d'art and extended to garden design and structures – visitors to Kew are reminded of the fashion by the pagoda, designed by Sir William Chambers after he had visited China and built in 1761.

The magnificence of China in the eighteenth century, in association with the traditional Chinese feeling of superiority towards foreigners, gave rise to an arrogance, and a mismatch of pretension and reality, which were to be prime causes of the misfortunes to follow. The flow of history can seldom be divided neatly into centuries, and stresses were building up behind the Manchu façade well before the nineteenth century began. A steep rise in population leading to pressure on cultivated land along with high inflation contributed to peasant unrest and to a recurrence of the phenomenon of rebellious secret societies with exotic names – the White Lotus and the Eight Trigrams. The late eighteenth century also saw an increase in corruption throughout government.

A great deal of later trouble might have been avoided if the Manchu Emperors could, while they were still riding high, have established relations of mutual respect and advantage with the European Powers. In 1793 a British Mission went to Peking to meet the Emperor. It was received with courtesy but made no real progress. The Emperor's reply to George III's message was distinctly discouraging, including the words "As your ambassador can see, we possess all things......and have no use for your country's manufactures." The Dutch East India Company sent a delegation to Peking two years later, but it was no more successful.

The mood was to darken. In 1816 Britain sent another mission, under Lord Amherst, who was expected to do homage to the Emperor by performing three genuflections and nine prostrations. Not surprisingly, Lord Amherst reacted robustly to this approach, and no progress was made. The European Powers and the United States did have limited facilities for trade, but in the absence of a sound diplomatic basis for the commercial activity there was frequent friction.

One of the largest areas of trade was the import of opium into China. The British East India Company shipped the drug in from India, a highly profitable venture. The Chinese authorities were, very understandably, alarmed at the debilitating effect of this trade on their people.

In 1833 the monopoly of the British East India Company was not renewed by Parliament, and a "free for all" began, with independent merchants determined to take a share of the opium trade. They were even more brazen than the British East India Company, which had shown some restraint because of the hostility of much opinion in Britain to such an immoral commercial activity.

Matters drifted towards open conflict and in 1839 began the first of those unhappy episodes in British foreign policy, the

Opium Wars. The first Opium War was launched by a Whig administration with Melbourne as Prime Minister and Palmerston as Foreign Secretary. Two contrasting views are sometimes heard on this Opium War and similar events. The first is that we cannot judge such events by the standards we might use today as such judgement would be anachronistic. The second, usually advanced by those who take a different political view, is that such unfortunate episodes should be regarded as in some sense typical of imperialism.

These views are difficult to sustain. Palmerston's policy was subject to severe criticism at the time on the basis of arguments which might be used today; an Anti-Opium League was formed which included Members of Parliament. Gladstone, then a Conservative, called the opium trade "infamous and atrocious" and wrote "I am in dread of the judgements of God upon England for our national iniquity towards China." When Britain became responsible for the government of a country the situation was very different from that which obtained in China, as notably illustrated by its involvement in India which is described later.

The first Opium War was unequal: the Chinese were no match for the British forces. In 1842 the War was concluded by the Treaty of Nanking under which five Treaty Ports were opened to British trade and removed from Chinese jurisdiction; Hong Kong Island was ceded. Where Britain had led, other countries followed in a scramble for trade and influence. Chinese resentment was deep.

In 1850 the T'ai-ping Rebellion broke out, fuelled by xenophobia, poverty and confused religious fanaticism. The rebellion was eventually put down with some help from outside, most notably from the then Major (later General) Gordon who became known as "Chinese Gordon" and was to die in 1885 when Khartoum was overrun by the forces of the

Mahdi. The sheer scale of slaughter in the Chinese Civil Wars of this time is not easy to comprehend. It is estimated that the T'ai-ping Rebellion, concentrated in the south, and the Nian Rebellion in the north together led to the loss of 25 million lives; and there were other risings, especially by Moslems.

In some aspects of life the advance of the nineteenth century showed an increasing influence of civilised, humanitarian values. In relations between the foreign powers and China, however, things went from bad to worse. The opium trade continued and a new, and now virtually forgotten, form of discreditable trade developed: the shipping of Chinese labour, under conditions of virtual slavery, to work on the sugar plantations of Cuba (then a Spanish possession) and in the mines of South America and California.

In late 1856 what is known as the second Opium War was precipitated when a British-registered ship, the Arrow, which was engaged in the opium trade, was boarded by the Chinese authorities. Palmerston, by now Prime Minister, wished to open hostilities. France agreed to participate. Napoleon III was not a person to neglect the possibility of a foreign military adventure, and the gruesome torture and murder of a French missionary, Father Chapdelaine, earlier in the year, provided a motive, or perhaps a pretext, for France to become involved.

Initial action by British forces aroused considerable disquiet at home. Palmerston faced a vote of censure in the House of Commons because of his policy towards China; the vote was carried with 263 in favour and 247 against. Palmerston dissolved Parliament and won the subsequent election. His victory in that election – albeit determined on the issue of general confidence in his leadership rather than the intricacies of policy towards China – certainly gave him a mandate for further military action.

During the subsequent war Canton was taken by British and French forces and in May 1858, in an action which established a precedent to be followed in 1900, British and French forces attacked the Taku forts at the mouth of the Pei Ho river, which guarded the route to Tientsin and, from there, to Peking. Following the seizure of the forts, the allies advanced as far as Tientsin. A series of agreements – known as the Treaties of Tientsin – between China and Britain, France, the United States and Russia involved Chinese acceptance of various concessions including diplomatic representation at Peking, the future significance of which scarcely needs to be pointed out.

This Treaty did not lead to peace. The Chinese strengthened the fortifications at Taku in what could be considered either prudent self-protection or bad faith according to one's point of view, and in the summer of 1859, after an initial repulse, an Anglo-French force once again forced its way past Taku. The rights and wrongs of the confused events of that time could still be debated. Methods of communication were quite primitive by the standards of the following century and people with civil or military authority, Chinese or Allied, often had to take decisions on their own initiative – in some cases, perhaps, gladly, in others reluctantly. However that may be, in March 1860 the scene was set for a new round of fighting when Britain sent an ultimatum to Peking demanding the admission of its envoy with proper ceremony. August 1860 saw Anglo-French forces again at Tientsin; this time they advanced to Peking. The city was taken, the Emperor fled and the Summer Palace was looted and burned. The Chinese were obliged to sign the Convention of Peking reinforcing the terms imposed in 1858. Vaughan makes reference to this campaign, which was evidently well recalled in 1900.

The years between 1860 and 1900 saw a scramble by

foreign powers for advantage in China. The Manchu court and the imperial bureaucracy had what one might describe as an intermittent understanding of the need for reform and for learning from what was at that time evident Western superiority in technology and social and political organisation. Progress was slow, however, hampered by decadence, intrigue and what we should now call denial. China was to suffer further dire blows before, by the end of the twentieth century, its self-respect and place in the community of nations was to be restored.

Unlike China, Japan had been eager to learn from the West, and one of the results was a conclusive Japanese victory in the war of 1894 between the two nations.

By 1900, the weakness of China had led to extensive foreign "spheres of influence" and to the concession to foreign powers of bases along the coast. In the north, Russian influence was strong in Manchuria and in 1898 Russia had leased Port Arthur. The British had established themselves in Weihaiwei, towards the eastern tip of the Shantung Peninsula, and the Germans at Kiaochow (Tsingtao) further to the south, with rights to build railways and develop mines in Shantung. Further south again, Shanghai, while not formally a British possession, was the centre of a zone of British influence which stretched west along both banks of the Yangtse. Opposite Formosa (Taiwan), annexed by Japan in 1895, Foochow and Amoy, not formally leased, provided the basis of a Japanese zone of influence. The British were at Hong Kong, the Portuguese at Macao and the French at Kuang-chou Wan. From there and from Annam and Laos, by now consolidated, along with Cambodia, into French Indo-China, French influence spread north across a swathe of Southern China.

It is scarcely surprising that this degree of foreign intrusion should give rise to popular discontent. The Boxers –

so called by foreigners because of their ritualised gestures – were in the tradition of Chinese popular movements to which reference has already been made. Xenophobia was an element in their world view; poverty fuelled their fanaticism.

The origin of the Boxer movement has been much debated. However deep the movement's roots, the effect of the Boxers could be described as more like a brushfire than a slow smoulder. It was the repressive policy of the Germans in Shantung whose punitive expeditions destroyed whole villages, which provided the tinder – if a date and place can be given for the start of the Boxer Rising, it is 1898 in Shantung; from there it spread rapidly.

The anger of the Boxers fell especially on foreign missionaries. This may be difficult to understand. The missionaries were sincere people; they brought practical benefits, for example Western medicine, as well as, in their perception, a hopeful spiritual message. Where the values of missionaries clashed with those of the Chinese it seems self-evident, at least in some instances, that missionary values were right. There was, for example, a widespread Chinese practice of female infanticide. The establishment of orphanages to save these little children was one of the activities of the missionaries.

Some Chinese were indeed converted to Christianity. Others, however, saw things from an entirely different perspective. Although Chinese religious beliefs were something of an amalgam, they were strongly held; in particular the worship of ancestors. Christian rejection of central Chinese beliefs could be seen as challenging traditional family and community values. Furthermore some missionaries – most notably French Roman Catholic – insisted on trappings of rank which identified them all too closely with hated foreign oppression.

The Boxer Movement could almost certainly have been quickly suppressed given resolute action by the Chinese Government. Such action was not forthcoming; to understand why one needs to consider the situation at the Manchu court and, in particular, the rôle of that central, enigmatic figure, Tzu Hsi, the Empress Dowager.

Yehonala (her Manchu name: Tzu Hsi was her official Chinese name with the meaning "Motherly and Auspicious") joined the court as the concubine of the Emperor Hsien-feng (1851-61). She gained so much influence that she became Regent on the death of Hsien-feng and the succession of their young son T'ung-chih. Two years after his succession in 1872 T'ung-chih died, and Tzu Hsi contrived the succession of her infant nephew Kuang-hsu, thereby resuming her career as Regent which she was very reluctant to abandon even when Kuang-hsu reached his majority in 1887. When Kuang-hsu asserted himself in the interests of reform, Tzu Hsi had him imprisoned in September 1898; he never recovered power.

Tzu Hsi, therefore, was a survivor. She did not at that time see it as her rôle to adapt China to the modern world; had she taken a different view, China might never have become a republic. If we think of her not just as a survivor but as a realist, it is difficult to interpret her attitude to the Boxers. Perhaps she really believed, at least for a while, that they possessed the magical power of invulnerability to bullets which they claimed, and could drive the foreigners out. It is also possible that from her knowledge of Chinese history she concluded that a popular movement of this nature might overthrow her unless she bent with the wind. Not surprisingly, foreigners in China failed to judge accurately her likely course of action.

An example of the baffling course of events is the development of the situation in Shantung where, as mentioned, the Boxer Rising started. In October 1899 there was an attack by Boxers on Christians in that province which was put down by Government troops. The Governor, Yu Hsien, dismissed the officials involved, giving the Boxers a green light, but was transferred under foreign pressure to Shansi, where he presided over a massacre of missionaries. He was replaced in Shantung by General Yuan Shih-k'ai who had proved his loyalty to Tzu Hsi by betraying to her the plans of the Emperor Kuang-hsu and the reformers in 1898. He might have been expected to go along with Tzu Hsi's favourable view of the Boxers but, instead, took measures to suppress the Rising. He was not supported by the Peking Government, and retreated into a neutral position towards the Boxers.

As to the subsequent course of the Rising, and the Siege of the Legations, space permits only a brief outline here. The nineteenth century ended with much of Northern China in chaos. There had been famine and the Yellow River had flooded; there was little effective Government help. The Boxers were able to exploit popular discontent and turn it against foreigners. An English missionary, the Reverend Sidney Brook, was killed on 31 December 1899. Although his murderers were executed, this represented a rare assertion of authority by the Imperial Court which – while subject to divided counsels – leaned heavily towards appeasement of, and collaboration with, the Boxers.

There was rising alarm within the Foreign Legations. The Legations, their presence in Peking a legacy of the 1860 war, were housed together and were – piquantly in view of the events of 1900 – neighbours of the Imperial Court. The force of events meant that the Legations had to make common cause against an external threat, but needless to say there was much

*A Boxer. The wording on his banner may be translated "By Imperial Decree the Righteous Harmonious Regiment Commissariat"*

rivalry as the individual Legations jockeyed for position in the interests of the Powers they represented.

Sir Claude MacDonald, the British Minister, the possessor of a splendid handlebar moustache, was a former soldier who had taken part, as had Vaughan, in the Egyptian Expedition of 1882. Edwin Conger, the American Minister, was also a former soldier – he had served in the Civil War. The United States had been flexing its muscles, as a liberator or imperial power according to one's interpretation, in Cuba and the Philippines; it wished to see China open to free trade but had no territorial ambitions there. A third former soldier, Baron von Ketteler the German Minister was, unhappily for him, to play a catalytic rôle in the unfolding drama. The French Minister, M. Pichon, was a politician, diplomat and colonial administrator. The Russian Minister, de Giers, showed himself more trusting of Chinese intentions than his colleagues in the Diplomatic Corps. The Japanese Minister, Baron Nishi, who spoke only his own language and Russian, does not appear to have carried great weight in the discussions within the Corps.

These were the men primarily responsible for confronting the developing crisis without the benefit of the modern systems of instant communication which we take for granted. As the situation deteriorated in the early part of 1900 the Ministers showed what seems in retrospect to have been a surprising complacency. It was a religious leader, Bishop Favier, Catholic Vicar-Apostolic of Peking, who really sounded the alarm. He warned the French Minister that unless action was taken there would be a massacre of Europeans and Chinese Christians in Peking.

On 20th May the Ministers considered Bishop Favier's representations and decided not to send for guards for the Legations but, instead, to make a renewed approach to the Chinese Government to persuade it to suppress the Boxers. By

$28^{th}$ May, however, the Ministers had decided to send for guards. The railway line from Tientsin, where allied forces were established, was still open and a contingent of guards from America, Britain, Russia, France, Italy, Japan, Germany and Austria arrived safely. The scene was set for the Siege of the Legations.

While tension remained at a high level in Peking, anxiety about the fate of the Legations led to the launching on $10^{th}$ June of a Relief Expedition under the leadership of Admiral Seymour. Bearing in mind that the guards for the Legations had travelled safely from Tientsin to Peking, it was not unreasonable to think that this larger force could follow the same route and ensure the safety of the Legations. The Boxers however sabotaged the railway line and made fanatical attacks on the expedition's trains. Meanwhile Tientsin had come under attack by regular Chinese troops. Seymour's force had itself to be rescued by an Allied sortie from Tientsin. Seymour's efforts had ended in a gallant failure; elsewhere there had been a spectacular success.

The Taku Forts represented a formidable threat to the Allied forces in Northern China. Controlling as they did the entrance to the Pei Ho river, the four forts had been modernised and their armament included Krupp guns. After their ultimatum demanding surrender of the forts had been answered by a bombardment directed at their ships, the Allied Admirals ordered an attack which, by bravery and luck, secured the Forts. This was a turning point in the Boxer crisis.

The fall of the Taku Forts had a dramatic effect in Peking. On $17^{th}$ June the Legations received an ultimatum from the Tsungli Yamen (Foreign Ministry) which said that, because of the demand by the Powers for surrender of the Taku Forts, the Diplomatic Corps, with guards, should leave for Tientsin within twenty-four hours. At a long meeting, only von Ketteler was adamant for rejecting the ultimatum; the majority view was for accepting it but asking for an extension of time. When no answer was forthcoming from the Chinese, von Ketteler set off to demand one. On the way a Bannerman – that is a member of the Chinese regular forces, not a Boxer – rushed from the crowd and shot him.

There was, and has continued to be, much speculation as to who gave orders for this murder if, indeed, it was not a spontaneous act. The effect of the murder was, however, unambiguous. The diplomats decided that if they left the Legation Quarter they would be walking into a trap. Defensive measures were taken and by the afternoon of 20$^{th}$ June the siege had begun.

After the failure of the Seymour Expedition, so-called after its leader, it was obvious that the forces at Tientsin would need substantial reinforcement before another effort to relieve the Legations could be made. There was much confusion in the outside world about the situation in Northern China and, needless to say, some suspicion and jockeying for position between the Powers who would have to take action. It was clearly necessary, however, for a further expedition to be mounted quickly, and the necessary forces were mustered. *St George and the Chinese Dragon* starts with the 7$^{th}$ Rajputs "warned for active service" on 19$^{th}$ June.

Before subsequent events are outlined, however, some account seems necessary to sketch in the Indian background, for to the modern eye it may seem strange that the greater part of the "British" element of the Relief Expedition should consist of Indian troops.

As in the case of China, the prime motivation for early European involvement with India was trade. This developed during the reign (1556-1605) of Akbar, considered the greatest of the Mughal Emperors – a dynasty of Mongol origin, Mughal being the Persian word for Mongol. The Portuguese were at first the leading European trading nation in India, but the foundation of the British East India Company in 1600 was a portent of how things were to develop. The Mughal Empire flourished under Akbar's successors Jahangir and Shah Jehan, but the religious fanaticism of Aurangzeb (reigned 1658-1707) – reversing the previously tolerant attitude of this Moslem dynasty towards Hinduism – sowed the seeds of the destruction of the Mughal Empire. The founding of the French East India Company in 1664 set the scene for a conflict between Britain and France for supremacy in an India which was in a disunited and confused state as Mughal power weakened. This conflict was effectively resolved by Robert Clive's victories during the 1750s, culminating in the Battle of Plassy (1757) which overthrew Siraj-ud Daula, the Nawab of Bengal, and put in his place a mere puppet of the East India Company. The French were expelled from Bengal, the beginning of the end for France's ambitions in India; the "private empire" of the East India Company went from strength to strength.

It was thus the British East India Company, not the British Government, which laid the foundations of what became the Indian Empire, but inevitably the Government became increasingly involved, establishing in 1784 a system of "dual control". The Company, under this arrangement, came under the supervision of a Board of Control whose President was a Cabinet Member responsible to Parliament. This system survived until 1857, when the outbreak known as the Indian Mutiny, which did indeed start as a mutiny on the part of "native" troops, but soon became much more, although it was always appreciably short of a national uprising, forced a fundamental rethink. In 1858 Company rule was ended and the Governor-General became the Viceroy; the office of Secretary of State for India replaced that of President of the Board of Control.

The rule of the British East India Company, and that of the British Government which succeeded it, were obviously of great significance for the development of India; but they also came to be important for the way the British saw themselves. It is perhaps still too early to take a fully measured view of the Raj, as it was known. Certainly, there was an unsavoury side to British involvement in India, especially in the early days. However for many British people the Raj came to represent not just an exotic adventure, and a career prospect, but also a vehicle for idealism. The British in India were in a situation quite different from the unfortunate one which, as outlined, existed in China. In India there was, at the best, a sense of responsibility by the British towards the indigenous population, vast and religiously-divided as it was; and a political, administrative, legal, military and social system was established which required a measure of consent and in which there was much mutual respect between the different elements.

One of the prime symbols of the system was the Indian Army. From 1668 to 1858 this was the British East India Company's army. Opportunities were provided for ambitious British officers; Arthur Wellesley, later Duke of Wellington, held senior commands in India between 1798 and 1805, experience which was valuable when he came to confront the armies of Napoleonic France. As early as 1762 the Indian Army was being deployed away from India, troops from Madras participating in that year in a British expedition which captured Manila in the Spanish Philippines. However, right up to and indeed beyond 1858 the Indian Army was seen as being for the defence, broadly interpreted, of the Indian Empire, not of the whole British Empire.

Early in the experience of the rival European Powers in India it was evident that Indian troops, when well led, equipped and trained, could be a match for European troops. The Indian

Army grew from this understanding. When things were at their best, good leadership by British officers evoked strong loyalty and created a powerful fighting force; an entity which drew Hindus, Moslems and Sikhs into working with a common purpose. However, there was an element of illusion in the system – the idea of British invincibility. The British in India may have been formidable but, in the final analysis, they were prone to the misjudgement and failure which are part of the human condition.

Vaughan's regiment, the 7$^{th}$ Rajputs, can be traced back through various titles to the eighteenth century Bengal Army. This was one of three regional groupings of the Indian Army, the others being Madras and Bombay, which corresponded to civil administrative divisions, or Presidencies. Although the Indian Mutiny took place mainly in the Bengal Army, the 47$^{th}$ Bengal Native Infantry, as the regiment was then called, remained loyal.

In 1880 Vaughan joined, as a young officer, a regiment then known as the 100$^{th}$ Foot based in Bengal – British regiments served alongside Indian Army ones as part of the defence forces of the Raj. The son of a clergyman, Vaughan was educated at Charterhouse and Rossall School. His military career started with the Northamptonshire and Rutland Militia; the duties were such as to allow him time to attend the Slade School, the recently-opened School of Fine Art of University College London, developing skills which he would put to good use later.

If, as seems likely from his subsequent career, Vaughan went to India seeking action and adventure, he was not to be disappointed. A few months after he joined the 7$^{th}$ Bengal Native Infantry – the then designation of the regiment which became the 7$^{th}$ Rajputs – in March 1882, there was a crisis in Egypt.

This crisis had been in the making since Arabi Pasha, a nationalist army officer, had seized effective power in February 1881 as a protest against the semi-colonial status into which Egypt had fallen under British and French influence. It boiled up when in June 1882 a riot in Alexandria led to the death of some fifty foreigners. This was thought likely to presage anarchy in Egypt, and when Arabi started to strengthen the Alexandria port defences the gun emplacements were bombarded by British warships. Further action was thought necessary and an army of 15,000 troops from Britain and 10,000 from India was dispatched under the overall command of Sir Garnet Wolseley; the 7th Rajputs were part of the Indian Army contingent.

The troops from Britain were shipped down the Suez Canal and occupied Ismailia on 19th August. The Indian contingent arrived at Suez itself, at the southern end of the Suez Canal, at the end of August, and Vaughan was dispatched to Ismailia. Wolseley's intention was to advance on Cairo; barring the way was Arabi's army in a fortified position at Tel-el-Kebir. The position was taken in a dawn attack. Vaughan painted a scene of the 7th Rajputs and the Seaforth Highlanders charging the enemy. This painting was, unhappily, destroyed by white ants while the regiment was in Burma, but a photograph of it is reproduced in the book by Sir Henry Rawlinson mentioned in the bibliography. The attack was a success and Cairo occupied; the authority of the Khedive, who had been, as we should say nowadays, marginalised by Arabi, was restored – naturally under strong British influence.

Vaughan's qualities of initiative, endurance and acute observation must have come to the attention of senior officers for he is to be found later in the decade involved in daring Intelligence work; a participant, indeed, in the Great Game. This term was used to describe the rivalry of Russia and Britain in Central Asia. As Tsarist Russia expanded towards India the

British, and particularly the British in India, took alarm at Russian intentions and contemplated, if that is not too passive a term, the possibility of a Russian invasion of India itself.

In 1885 matters came close to outright war between Britain and Russia because of the Russian seizure of the oasis of Pandjeh, on the road to Herat in Afghanistan. The crisis was defused but the rivalry continued over a wide band of territory which included Persia. The Shah Nasir ad-Din was basically sympathetic to Britain, but had to take account of Russian power on his northern border. Britain was concerned that Russian influence in Persia posed a threat to India via Afghanistan, but did not wish to be provocative. Sir Henry Drummond Wolff, appointed Minister to Teheran in 1888, sought to strengthen Persia and saw merit in co-operation with Russia.

In December 1887 Vaughan arrived in Persia to begin the first of two remarkable journeys in that country. His account of the first journey was read at the Royal Geographical Society on 10th March 1890 by Major-General Sir Frederic Goldsmid, and the President of the Society said at the end of the meeting that "they had reason to be grateful to Lieut. Vaughan for having undertaken a journey in so very dreary a country simply for the purpose of increasing human knowledge."

It is, perhaps, scarcely necessary to say that matters were not as simple as that. In addition to a paper for the Royal Geographical Society, Vaughan prepared a *Report of a Journey through Persia* for the Intelligence Branch of the Quarter Master General's Department in India, which was printed with a confidential heading. Vaughan was, in fact, engaged in what might tactfully be described as intelligence work, and the formidably detailed account he gives in his *Report* includes much of direct military relevance – there are a number of references, for example, to whether roads are passable by guns.

From his starting point on the Persian Gulf, Vaughan travelled north through mountain territory up to Yezd, after which he skirted the Great Salt Desert (Dasht-I-Kavir), turning to the east before he reached Teheran. His account for the Royal Geographical Society leaves him, rather mysteriously, at Gunabad, near the Caspian Sea. In his *Report* for Intelligence Branch he reveals a subsequent adventure. From Gunabad Vaughan travelled to Bandar Ghez on the Caspian. He then contrived to board a Russian ship: "Some Naval officers are employed on it, and one used always to inspect the ticket", Vaughan wrote. The ship called at Baku – about 20 steamers in harbour, Vaughan noted, and at a port close to the mouth of the Volga, with "numerous barges and floating landing stages" from where "large well-fitted flat-bottomed river steamers ran up the Volga. They are paddle boats, with two decks, and are capable of carrying each about 800 to 1,000 men, with baggage and stores." The implication was clear: Vaughan was assessing this site as a potential launching-point for a Russian force which might threaten India.

In 1890-91 Vaughan undertook another, even more remarkable, journey in Persia, an account of which appeared in the Geographical Journal for 1896. The initial part of the journey, as far as Yezd, was similar to that of 1887. After that he criss-crossed the Great Salt Desert. On this journey he had company for part of the way. Near Isfahan he met an old friend, Captain (later Brigadier-General) Edmund Burton, and did a west-east crossing of the Desert to Tabbas. In 1957, when Robin Hanbury-Taylor visited Tabbas, he was told that only four Europeans had visited in the last 200 years. Vaughan and Burton returned along the northern fringe of the desert following a similar route to Vaughan's on his 1887-88 journey, but in the opposite direction. At Teheran Vaughan parted from Burton, and travelled to Isfahan with C.E. Biddulph of the India Civil Service, who described their journey together in his book

*Four Months in Persia* although – no doubt for security reasons – Vaughan is not named, nor are any personal details given.

For his explorations in Persia Vaughan was awarded the MacGregor Medal in 1892. This Medal was founded in 1888 as a memorial to Sir Charles MacGregor, a formidable soldier, advocate of a "forward policy" towards Russia, and first head of the Indian Army's Intelligence Department. It was awarded annually for the best military reconnaissance in or adjacent to India – it could have been described as the medal of the Great Game. Other recipients included Francis Younghusband (1890) later the commander of the 1904 British Expedition to Tibet, and Orde Wingate (1943) for leading the first Chindit expedition in Japanese-occupied Burma.

Burma was to feature in Vaughan's career also, for while he was on his second journey in Persia the $7^{th}$ Rajputs left India (April 1891) for service in Upper Burma, where conditions were unsettled following its annexation on $1^{st}$ January 1886 as a result of the third Burmese War, when Britain had moved from regarding Burma as a "buffer state" to a policy of direct rule. Vaughan, who had been designated as officiating Second in Command when the $7^{th}$ Rajputs were sent to Burma, must have joined his regiment at some point after he left Persia around the end of June 1891, although detailed information about his rôle in Burma is lacking.

Vaughan, seasoned not only in command but in reporting, was well qualified not only to lead the $7^{th}$ Rajputs on the Relief Expedition but also to write the account which was published as *St George and the Chinese Dragon*. It will not be a purpose of this Introduction to steal Vaughan's thunder, so to speak, by giving an account of the Relief Expedition; readers who would like another account may consult one of the books listed in the bibliography which cover the ground. However, after this

25

diversion, remote as it has been from Peking in 1900, it is time to return to the besieged Legations.

Aspects of the course of the Siege of the Legations were baffling to the besieged and have been scarcely less so to historians. It is difficult to exaggerate the gravity and recklessness of the course on which the Chinese Government had embarked. Respect for the safety of the emissaries of foreign powers is deeply ingrained in diplomacy and goes back to ancient times: the principle was being violated. The retribution which would have followed a massacre of the defenders of the Legations would have been formidable; imperial rule would almost certainly have been brought to an end and China might have ceased to exist as a sovereign state, partitioned between the Powers.

It is scarcely surprising, therefore, that there were divided counsels on the Chinese side. A crucial factor in the failure of the siege appears to have been the attitude of Jung Lu, the Commander in Chief, who was opposed to the Boxers and the attack on the Legations. This does not mean that the defenders of the Legations were wrong to perceive themselves to be in real and imminent danger. If Jung Lu was what we should now call a dove, there were a number of hawks. The figurehead of the war party was Prince Tuan, who had a virulent dislike of foreigners. His appointment as President of the Tsungli Yamen (Foreign Ministry) on 10$^{th}$ June had been an ominous development.

The Legations were defended by guards of eight nationalities, the total strength being 20 officers and 389 other ranks with some support by volunteers. Although there was a shortage of ammunition, the defenders of the Legations were in other respects reasonably well equipped. The lack of a properly unified command nearly led to disaster only two days into the siege after an Austrian naval officer, Captain von Thomann, who lacked relevant experience but had seniority, ordered the abandonment of much of the defended area after he had received misleading information. This was reversed before the Chinese had taken full advantage of the opportunity given, and Sir Claude MacDonald, who as already mentioned was a former army officer, took over command.

Days of fierce fighting were interrupted by what appears to be a peace overture by the Chinese Government; nothing came of it, no doubt because of the struggle for influence which was taking place at Tzu Hsi's court. The siege settled into a grim pattern. Casualties mounted and conditions in the makeshift hospital were bad. Ground was lost to the besieging forces but counter-attacks took place. The Chinese started to erect a small fort close to the American position on the Tartar Wall. On 3$^{rd}$ July a force of some fifty Americans, Britons and Russians under the command of Captain Myers of the American marines succeeded in taking the fort in a confused battle. At the opposite corner of the defended area, the Japanese were resolute in their defence of the area known as the Fu; their commander, Colonel Shiba the Military Attaché, was the outstanding military figure of the siege, and the high opinion which Colonel Vaughan expressed in *St George and the Chinese Dragon* of the soldierly quality of the Japanese corresponds to the views expressed by survivors of the siege.

By Friday 13$^{th}$ July, described by Sir Claude MacDonald as "the most harassing day for the defence during the whole course of the siege" the position had deteriorated considerably. The Japanese defenders of the Fu, supported by Italians, had been forced back almost to their last line of defence; the Germans, supported by the Russians, had to resort to a bayonet-charge to restore their position; two mines exploded under the French Legation. On 16$^{th}$ July Captain Strouts, the Royal Marine officer who not only commanded the British contingent but acted, in effect, as MacDonald's Chief of Staff, was killed.

The attrition of death, injury and exhaustion was severely weakening the defence. The situation was desperate, but surrender was regarded as out of the question.

Meanwhile, the Allied forces at Tientsin, assembling in preparation for the Relief Expedition, had, after some delay, begun their advance. After an attack during which the Japanese played the decisive part, turning potential failure into success, the walled city of Tientsin was taken. As the fall of the Taku Forts had precipitated the Legation siege, the collapse of resistance at Tientsin, stern warnings from the Powers, and dissent from the anti-foreign campaign by senior Chinese regional officials, brought a remission to the ordeal of the besieged in Peking. On 17$^{th}$ July the Chinese Government declared a truce in Peking; for a while the doves were in the ascendant and, in a bizarre development, gifts of melons and other food arrived at the Legation Quarter as a gift from the Empress.

The truce was not to last. As the commanders of the Allied forces at Tientsin debated their next step, Li Ping-heng, a favourite of Tzu Hsi and a leading hawk, arrived at Peking and was appointed Deputy Commander of the Northern Armies. There was a purge of those who favoured peace, and the stage was set for the final phase of the siege of the Legations.

From 29$^{th}$ July, when hostilities restarted, until 13$^{th}$ August, the Legations were under less intense pressure than they had been before the truce. Furthermore, reliable information was at last arriving from outside. Elsewhere in Peking, however, there was neither truce nor easing of pressure. Bishop Favier, whose warning to the Legations has been mentioned earlier, had provided at the Peitang Cathedral sanctuary for more than three thousand men, women and children, of whom the great majority were Chinese Christians. They were defended by forty-three French and Italian sailors;

their commander was the 23-year-old Paul Henry. Facing almost hopeless odds, Paul Henry – who died on the 30th July – and his small force conducted a defence in respect of which the term heroic can, even in this cynical age, be applied. After Henry's death the defenders were even more vulnerable than before, but the Chinese attackers seem by then to have lost stomach for the fight, although they did much damage by exploding mines.

On 13th August, with the Relief Expedition at Tungchow, the Chinese made a final effort to overrun the Legations. Every weapon in the Legation Quarter was distributed for what was shaping up to be a desperate battle. The sound of firing could be heard by the advancing Allies. The flags of Great Britain, the United States and Russia were hoisted on the Tartar Wall to guide the rescuers.

The Allies had a plan for their advance on Peking but, probably more because of confusion than bad faith, this went distinctly adrift. The Russians attacked before the agreed time an objective which had been allotted to the Americans, the Tung Pien Men (Gate). While this could be interpreted as a discreditable attempt to steal an advantage, from another point of view it could be said to show a very desirable sense of urgency in view of the dire situation at the Legations. However that may be, by the time the British forces had arrived at the walls of Peking the Chinese defenders were so heavily engaged on other sectors that they were able to offer only light resistance and, as described by Vaughan, it was to troops of the Indian Army that the honour fell of being the first to reach the Legations.

Vaughan's account of the Relief of the Legations and subsequent events require in my view no further comment or elaboration, except that the leading rôle in the rescue of those besieged at the Peitang Cathedral was played by the Japanese –

Vaughan's book, generous to the Japanese in other respects, fails to point that out.

Although we can attempt, for the sake of neatness, to draw a line under an historical event, the ramifications of events continue into the indefinite future. The Boxer Rising has resonances which reach to the present, and for that reason it is tempting to leave matters as does Vaughan, with a sense that the drama is over and it is time to move on. However the reader may be interested in a brief summary of subsequent events in China and some wider reflections.

Before that, however, reference should be made to Vaughan's life after China. The 7$^{th}$ Rajputs arrived back in India in September 1901. There were to be no further major adventures in Vaughan's service career, which ended as Commandant of the 7$^{th}$ Rajputs. He retired before the First World War and returned to England, where he was recalled to service in the British Army during that War. In 1922 he moved to Guernsey with his family and, along with his wife, played an active part in the life of the island. He developed there his interests as a painter and exhibited his work. He died in 1934; recording the event, regimental records said that "He was a gifted painter, a man of considerable ability, and a fine and gallant leader in the field." That may stand as his epitaph.

There is a reference in *St George and the Chinese Dragon* to the flight of Tzu Hsi as Peking was falling. In two carts, the Empress and her immediate entourage left Peking on an odyssey from which she was not to return until January 1902. During that time peace had been concluded, summary justice had been done, and the world's attention had moved elsewhere. Tzu Hsi's arrival back in Peking was ceremonial, unlike her flight. It was watched, from a balcony on the damaged Chien Men (Gate) by many members of the foreign community, to whom Tzu Hsi gave a little bow; they broke into applause.

Tzu Hsi had at last been convinced of the need for reform and there was a thorough-going modernisation. The Manchu dynasty did not, however, long survive her death in 1908. A republic was declared in 1911; civil war followed, first between the Nationalists (Kuomintang) and warlords – provincial rulers who, as in previous phases of Chinese history, took advantage of the weakening of central authority to establish their own irresponsible power. Civil war then broke out between Nationalists and Communists. A weakened China was vulnerable to Japanese aggression in the 1930s and Japanese troops left China only after the conflict between the two countries had been subsumed, so to speak, in the wider conflagration of the Second World War, when the Japanese surrendered after the dropping of nuclear bombs on Hiroshima and Nagasaki. After the Second World War the Communists won the civil war with the Nationalists and, after many vicissitudes, China approached the next millennium once again a great power. Modern Chinese, looking back at the humiliations of 1900, may well feel satisfaction at how far their country has come in a hundred years.

For the proud victors of 1900 the future was to hold much horror and great change. The tensions in Europe were to explode into the First World War, a convulsion which bred the evils of totalitarianism, and a Second World War after which the world community did, at last, seem to have taken to heart some lessons on the need to contain and reduce conflict.

At the time this Introduction is being written, soldiers of six of the nations which participated in the Relief Expedition – Russia, Britain, United States, France, Germany and Italy – are engaged together in peacekeeping in Kosovo. This is, of course, a very different type of enterprise from the Relief Expedition but throws up, perhaps, problems of co-ordination and of clarification of objectives which would not have been unfamiliar a hundred years ago.

While it is fashionable, and in many ways right, to strive to take a global rather than a national view, it would seem wrong to end this Foreword without making a specific reference to the rôle of Britain, and of the British Empire, in the events described in this book, and more generally. By 1900 some people were already wondering how long this Empire could last; Kipling in his *Recessional*, written in 1897, had dwelt on the possibility that the day would come when

Lo, all our pomp of yesterday
Is one with Nineveh and Tyre!

Such has, in a sense, been the fate of the British Empire, but when we reflect on the positive contributions which the Empire, for all its flaws, has made to the world we should perhaps end not with Kipling but with Tennyson, who in *Ulysses* reminded us

Tho' much is taken, much abides.

# India, China, Japan and adjacent countries in 1900

Legend:
- British
- French
- Dutch
- American
- Japanese

RUSSIAN EMPIRE

CHINESE

PERSIA

AFGHANISTAN

TIBET ○ Lhasa

NEPAL

BHUTAN

Delhi ○

INDIAN

EMPIRE

Calcutta ○

Arabian sea

○ Bombay

Bay of
Bengal

Ran

○ Goa (Portuguese)

Madras ○

ANDAMAN IS.
(British)

Indian Ocean

CEYLON

Colombo ○

NICOBAR IS.
(British)

Kota R

N

MALDIVE IS.
(British)

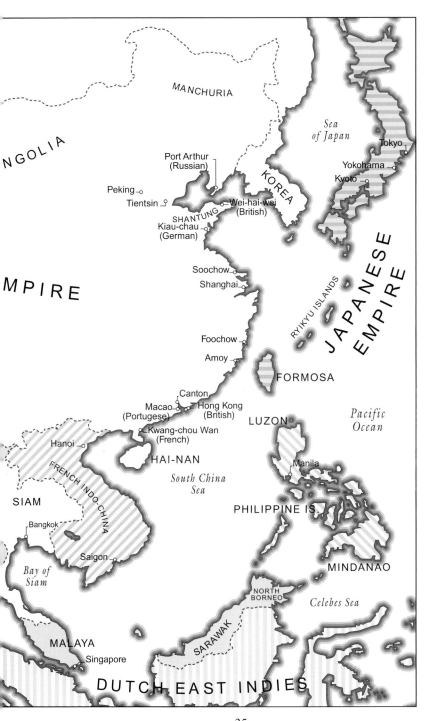

MANCHURIA

NGOLIA

*Sea of Japan*

Tokyo

Port Arthur (Russian)

KOREA

Yokohama

Kyoto

Peking

Tientsin

Wei-hai-wei (British)

SHANTUNG

Kiau-chau (German)

Soochow

Shanghai

MPIRE

J A P A N E S E   E M P I R E

RYIIKYU ISLANDS

Foochow

Amoy

FORMOSA

Canton

Macao (Portugese)

Hong Kong (British)

Kwang-chou Wan (French)

LUZON

*Pacific Ocean*

Hanoi

HAI-NAN

Manila

FRENCH INDO-CHINA

*South China Sea*

SIAM

PHILIPPINE IS.

Bangkok

Saigon

MINDANAO

*Bay of Siam*

NORTH BORNEO

*Celebes Sea*

MALAYA

SARAWAK

Singapore

DUTCH EAST INDIES

*Colonel Vaughan*

# Introduction

Having kept a diary during the advance on Pekin, I had begun to write it up for publication, when it occurred to me that a general account of the advance, which included the doings of the other corps present, would be more interesting to the public. The Officers commanding the 1$^{st}$ Sikhs and 24$^{th}$ Punjab Infantry, Lieut.-Colonels Pollock and Ramsay, have kindly supplied accounts of the movements of their regiments.

Most of the sketches* were made on the very ground where the incidents depicted occurred, and truthfulness was aimed at rather than artistic effect. My best thanks are due to Officers commanding corps, who have allowed me to make use of their men as models.

H. B.V.

*July* 1902

---

* Some sketches in the original edition have not been used in this one for technical reasons.

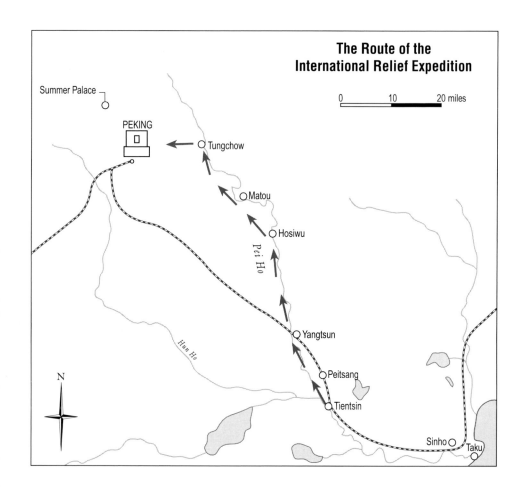

The Route of the
International Relief Expedition

Summer Palace

PEKING

Tungchow

Matou

Hosiwu

Pei Ho

Han Ho

Yangtsun

Peitsang

Tientsin

Sinho

Taku

N

0    10    20 miles

# CHAPTER I.

## AT DUTY'S CALL

The 7$^{th}$ Duke of Connaught's Own Bengal Infantry, known as the 7$^{th}$ Rajputs, stationed at Fort William, Calcutta, was warned for active service on June 19, 1900. We were to be re-armed with the Lee-Metford rifle* before sailing, and were to take a Maxim gun* with us. When this order arrived a large number of the men were on leave and furlough, and most of the British officers were away on various duties.

The regiment sailed for China in the British India Steam Navigation Company's ships *Nerbudda* and *Palamcotta*, which started, one on the 25$^{th}$, the other on the 29$^{th}$ of the same month.

After an uneventful voyage, we arrived off Taku on the 14$^{th}$ and 15$^{th}$ of July, and anchored close to the allied fleets, which numbered over thirty war vessels, and formed a magnificent sight. Amongst them lay a Chinese war-ship, the breech blocks and sights of whose guns had been considerably taken charge of by the admirals of the allied fleets. A remarkable ship was an American transport which had conveyed cavalry, and had two tiers of horse boxes built one above the other on the upper deck.

The naval transport officer came on board of us, and it was decided that we should embark in lighters, and be towed

---

* The Lee-Metford rifle and the Maxim gun were examples of the most up-to-date weapons technology in 1900. The rifle, a bolt action weapon with a six round magazine, had been adopted by the British Army in 1888 – the bolt action, by bringing a fresh cartridge into position as soon as the previous one had been used, facilitated a rapid rate of fire. The Maxim gun – named after its inventor, the American Hiram Maxim (1840-1916) – was a fully automatic machine gun and the first such weapon to be adopted (in 1887) by the British Army.

up the Peiho River to Tientsin on the following day. We had three months' stores on board, and the captain of the ship derided the idea of our being able to unload the vessel and fill the lighters in less than seventy-two hours. However, everybody set to work with a will, and by the afternoon of the next day we had loaded up and started.

Crossing the bar, we steamed up past the Taku Forts, on which the flags of the different nations were flying. The marines and blue-jackets turned out and cheered us as we passed a fort on our right, where our flag was flying. We passed several gunboats lying in the stream, manned by English and Russian crews, who all cheered. At Sinho, a few miles up the river, a light draught tug, armed with a Maxim in charge of blue-jackets, took us in tow. The river, very dirty and full of mud, was swift, and the banks were low, with rushes growing in many places. We steamed on long after darkness had set in, and then anchored in the stream.

Early on the 17$^{th}$ we got under way. As we progressed, we passed many dead bodies of Chinese in the river, and the stench was most unpleasant. At one point we met crowds of men, women, and children streaming along the road near the river bank. A Chinese sailor on board told us they were flying from the Russian troops; clouds of smoke were seen rising from burning villages on the left bank of the river.

Soon after, we passed two armed Russian soldiers moving through the crops by themselves, while the natives were flying in all directions from them. They appeared to be searching the houses, and to be trying to get close up to the Chinese to catch them, for if they had wanted to shoot them they could easily have done so, being within two or three hundred yards. I can only conclude that they were trying to catch some of their women, by no means a difficult job, as with their small deformed feet*, unless assisted, they can't possibly get away.

We passed villages burning by the water's edge. None of the people seemed to mind us at all, and in one place where we ran aground they brought us vegetables. The whole country is one level fertile plain, covered with luxuriant crops, and thickly studded with villages.

Towards midday we reached Tientsin, and to get to it had to pass the Russian bridge of boats, which opened to let us through. After lunch at the "Orlando" Mess, we were quartered in a large corrugated iron warehouse of Messrs. Jardine and Matheson on the left bank.

After leaving the sea we found the heat oppressive, and the warehouse was so hot during the middle of the day that the officers shifted into tents near it, which were much cooler. The noise, too, in the warehouse, with 350 Sepoys** in it, all talking at the same time, and each trying to talk louder than his neighbour, was simply deafening.

The other wing of the regiment arrived by rail from Sinho on the 18$^{th}$. We arrived at Tientsin two days after the last shot had been fired, and learnt to our surprise that the Legations at Pekin were still supposed to be holding out. We were busy for several days unloading the supplies in our lighters, during which we held parades, practising the men in the attack across country. They were told to use far more independent fire than is usual, and advancing by driblets from the flanks of companies, as well as by the whole company advancing simultaneously, was practised.

* The consequence of the practice, widespread in Imperial (i.e. pre-1911) China, of binding the feet of infant girls so as to produce, when the girls were fully grown, what were thought to be exquisitely small (and therefore attractive) feet.

** Sepoy was the basic rank in the Infantry of the Indian Army, equivalent to Private in the British Army.

There were many signs at Tientsin of the severe fighting that must have taken place. Houses were much damaged by shell fire, and barricades were still standing in many of the streets.

Tientsin was filling fuller every day with troops of all nationalities. We were warm friends with the Americans, and it was astonishing to see how well the troops of all the other Powers got along with each other. There was a large Russian encampment close to us, and their men were much interested in watching our Sepoys at their duties.

The Russians strike one as being a fine, sturdy, well-developed body of men, but there is considerable room for improvement in their sanitary arrangements. I was amused one day at seeing my old bearer (Hindu servant) in a field trying to dig up some vegetables. A burly Russian came along, and after watching for a time his efforts with his bare hands, promptly set to work, and dug up a quantity with his bayonet fixed on the end of his rifle, and handed them to him.

The Japanese are pleasant little men, always cheerful and happy looking, and very like the Ghurkas in appearance and manner. Our men mistook them for Ghurkas at first.

As time passed there were many conflicting rumours regarding the Legations at Pekin, and the general opinion gradually grew stronger that they must have fallen. It was rumoured at one time that the Boxers were advancing again on Tientsin City, and we were ordered to send out a picket of a hundred men. We posted night sentries round the north and west faces of our enclosure, and a lookout on a platform by day. The south face of our camp was protected by the river, and the east face by the Russian camp.

Preparations soon began for the advance on Pekin. Orders were issued that regiments were only to take 500 rifles, and the remainder of the men with two British officers from each regiment were to remain to garrison Tientsin.

It was interesting to see the crowd watching the drums and pipes of the 1$^{st}$ Sikhs while they played in front of their quarters - Russian, French, German, American, Japanese, and Italian officers and men were there in numbers. I doubt if any of them had ever heard the bagpipes before, or seen an Indian soldier.

Many rumours were current at this time. One was that General Gaselee was going to advance with his force and the Americans and Japanese, but that the others were unwilling to start, alleging that there were insufficient troops for the undertaking.

General Gaselee says in his despatches:

"On my arrival at Tientsin I at once put myself into communication with the general officers commanding the American and Japanese forces, and soon came to a satisfactory understanding. We decided to impress collectively upon the allied commanders the absolute necessity of pressing forward towards Pekin at the earliest possible moment, and happily our views were eventually accepted."

A boat column was formed, two boats being allotted to my regiment; these contained the field service, kits of officers and men, ten days' rations, and the second reserve of ammunition. No tents were taken. There were hospital boats, engineer boats, and others. A guard of four men was told off to each boat, and distinctive flags were hoisted on them. Ours carried a yellow flag, on which a large 7 was displayed.

The column consisted of about fifty-five boats; Commander G. Barrett, R.N., was naval officer in charge, and Captain H. O. Parr of the 7$^{th}$ Rajputs was in military charge.

There were boats also containing the naval 12-pounder quick-firing guns, and the 4-inch quick-firing gun; the guns belonging to the Hong-Kong Singapore Artillery were also carried by water during a portion of the advance.

Chinese coolies* were employed under a military guard to work the boats, which were poled and hauled up the river by them, and Japanese coolies were also employed on this work, but they occasionally proved obstreperous and quarrelsome. When this occurred, it was found that the best way of bringing them to reason was to fling them into the river, after which, on again reaching the boats, they resumed their work quietly, but for a short time only. Then the sterner persuasion of the stick was resorted to.

The boats had to be lightly laden, so as to draw not more than one and a half feet of water. There was also one steam-boat with the flotilla for towing hospital boats, but she proved to be of little or no use, and only got as far as Yangtsun. The length of the boat column was generally six miles. The following is a brief account of its advance:-

After the second march, that is, after leaving Yangtsun, the relieving force was marching on Pekin by a route that was straight as compared with the circuitous windings of the river; consequently the boats in order to keep up had to travel night and day. The river fell sixteen inches in one night while the boats were at Yangtsun, owing to the enemy having cut the river bank higher up. This caused great anxiety, as had the water continued to fall, the boats would have been unable to advance. The Japanese, however, discovered the breach and repaired it early next morning. There were also the boat-flotillas of other nationalities, and at difficult reaches, corners, &c., the boats of the various columns were mixed up, and the

*A term used for manual labourers in South and East Asia.

tow-lines twisted together, so that in some cases they had to be cut, which caused still further delay.

At Nuschia, some distance beyond Tsaisun, a Chinaman came and gave information that the river banks were mined. The boats were stopped, and the train to the mines was followed up to a temple in the village, where an electrical apparatus for discharging it was found. The train was taken up and carried away. Had the mines been exploded, as was the intention of the Chinese, the boats when passing them would have been sunk, forming an obstruction to the navigation, while the mines placed in the river bank would have blown it open and let out the water. The boats must have arrived at Tungchow some time on the $13^{th}$ of August, as Captain Parr rejoined us a few hours before we entered Pekin.

The composition of the Pekin relief force was, as nearly as can be ascertained, as shown on the following pages. The total force was approximately as follows :-

```
10,000  Japanese  with  24  guns.
 4,000  Russians    "   16   "
 3,000  British     "   12   "
 2,000  Americans   "    6   "
   800  French      "   12   "
   100  Austrians and Italians.
        Total - 19,900, with 70 guns.
```

COMPOSITION OF THE PEKIN RELIEF FORCE.

BRITISH TROOPS.

*Commanding.*
A.D.C. Lieut.-General Sir A. Gaselee, K.C.B., S. C.

*Aides-de-camp.*
Capt. B. T. Pell, R. W. Surr. R.
Lieut. R. A. Steel, $17^{th}$ B. L.

*Chief of the Staff.*
Major-General E. G. Barrow, C.B., S. C.

*Assist. Adjt. and Q.M-G.*
Lieut.-Colonel G. H. O. Sullivan, R.E.

*Dep. Assist. Adjt. and Q.M.-G.*
Capt. I. Phillips, 1$^{st}$ Batt. 5$^{th}$ Gurkhas.

*Dep. Assist. Q.M.-G. for Intelligence*
Capt. E. W. M. Norie, Middlesex R.

*Commanding Royal Artillery.*
Major G. F. W. St. John, R.A.

*Commanding Royal Engineers.*
Lieut.-Colonel K. G. Scott-Moncreiff, R.E.

*Assistant Field Engineer.*
Lieut. S. G. Loch, R.E.

*Principal Medical Officer.*
Lieut.-Colonel Rainsford, R.A.M.C.

*Provost-Marshal.*
Capt. R. B. Low, D.S.O., 9$^{th}$ B. L.

*Chief Commissariat Officer.*
Major Koe, A.S.C.

1$^{ST}$ INFANTRY BRIGADE STAFF.
Major-General Sir Norman Stewart, Bart., S. C.

*Orderly Officer.*
Major A. W. Leonard, 5$^{th}$ Infantry, H. C.

*Dep. Asst. Adjt-General.*
Capt. T. Jermyn, 2$^{nd}$ Sikhs.

*Brigade Commissariat and Transport Officer.*
Capt. R. E. Vaughan, S.C.

# NAVAL BRIGADE

\* Blue-jackets, 140 men with four 12-pounder quick-firing guns.
† Royal Marine Light Infantry, 300 rifles.


## LAND FORCES.

No. 12 Battery Royal Field Artillery, 6 guns.
‡ Hong-Kong Singapore Artillery, two 12-pounder quick-firing guns, 12 cwt., mounted on captured Krupp carriages drawn by mules, and driven by Japanese coolies engaged as soldiers. Four Maxims.
Detachment Royal Engineers.
1$^{st}$ Bengal Lancers, 400.
\* 2$^{nd}$ Battalion Royal Welsh Fusiliers, 300.
7$^{th}$ Rajputs, 500.
24$^{th}$ Punjab Infantry, 300.
1$^{st}$ Sikhs, 500.
\* Hong-Kong Regiment, 100.
\* Chinese Regiment,100.

Total – 3000 men, with 12 guns.


\* Present at Tientsin during the siege.

† Most of them were with Admiral Seymour during his attempt to relieve Pekin.

‡ These used smoke powder during the siege, and I hear that on one occasion they opened fire in the vicinity of a battery employing smokeless. This gave away the battery at once, and the enemies' shells immediately began to fall fast and thick about them. The Maxims were then politely asked to move a little farther off.

The United States Army consisted of the following troops:-

Commanding – General Chaffee.

12 Companies $9^{th}$ U.S. Infantry.

8　　　"　　　$14^{th}$ U.S.　"

2 Battalions U.S. Marines.

Light Battery "F" ("Riley's" $5^{th}$ U.S. Artillery), and detachment of Engineer, Signal, and Hospital Corps, U.S. Army.

1 Troop $6^{th}$ U.S. Cavalry.

Total – 2000 men, and 6 field guns.

Several reconnaissances were made towards Pei-tsang about the end of July and beginning of August, and from these it was ascertained that the enemy was in position with guns in considerable force in that direction.

The rains had apparently failed so far, but the question was – might they not break in August with an extra heavy downpour to make up for the deficiency during June and July? Several people who knew China well replied, in answer to inquiries, that they didn't see how any advance could take place till the autumn. "The rainy season will set in in a few days," they said, "and the whole place will be under water; the hollow roads by which you will have to advance will be full of water and mud." Others said that there were not enough troops to advance with, and that, were we to start, another expedition would have to be sent to relieve us; that we couldn't expect to get through with such a small force.

# CHAPTER II.

## THROUGH HOSTILE HORDES

At last the advance was ordered to take place, each officer and man to carry two days' reserve rations; the men had prepared theirs.

On the afternoon of August 4, 1900, headed by our drums and fifes, we marched out, crossed the Russian bridge, and fell in our place in the column as we passed the Temperance Hall. A few Europeans gathered to see us off.

We marched about four miles, passing through Tientsin native city. Then heavy rain fell for a short time. We bivouacked in a field behind an embankment; no fires were allowed. General Sir A. Gaselee, at his quarters in the village close by, explained to us the plan of attack for the next day.

From the reconnaissances already referred to, and other information, the Chinese were believed to occupy a strong position near Pei-tsang astride the Pei-ho. It was decided to force this position, and push on to Yangtsun, so as to secure the passage of the river at that important strategical point. We, *i.e.* the British, were to form the second line of the left column of the allied forces operating on the right bank of the Pei-ho River - first line, Japanese; second line, British and American forces: Americans on the right, British on the left. Object, to turn the enemy's right flank. Movement might commence at 1 A.M., but the British force would probably not be required to move till about 3 A.M., but to be ready to move at 2 A.M.

After a scratch dinner we lay down; regiment in column of companies in front, officers and hospital next, and mules in rear. Rain fell during the night, and it wasn't at all pleasant.

49

Saddles were used as pillows, and with our great-coats spread over us we lay on the bare ground. Our doctor, however, was in clover, as he slept in his hospital doolie, a litter to carry a man lying at full length, with a waterproof roof and curtains. We stood to arms at 1.30 A.M. on 5$^{th}$ August, and finally marched at 4 A.M., along a track on the south side of the bund embankment. Firing was heard ahead of us to our right front; the rattle of musketry and booming of big guns, which as we advanced grew louder.

Dawn now commenced, and I saw one or two men of the 1$^{st}$ Sikhs and 24$^{th}$ P.I.* who were leading sitting down by the roadside pressing their hands to their legs or arms. When I asked them what was the matter, they said they had been hit by bullets. I then realised that we were under fire; wounded Japanese soldiers began to stream past, and dead horses were passed lying on the roadside.

After going some distance we were ordered to halt, and lay down on the south slope of the embankment and charged magazines. Our field-battery now came up, and we closed to the right to make room for them. Two gunners came up and began taking the range. I stood up and looked over the embankment to see what object they were taking the range to. At that moment a shell whirred past me, and burying itself in the ground about ten yards behind, burst with a dull report in the high crops. "A narrow shave that, sir," remarked one of the range-takers, who was close alongside.

I went and lay down on the left of our line. A few minutes after an officer of the Hong Kong Regiment came up and said, "Three of your men are lying wounded just behind you." I went down and looked, and saw three of our signallers lying on the ground groaning, and saying, "Gole laga, doctor bhejdo" - "We are wounded, send a doctor." Our doctor arrived, then the

* Punjab Infantry

battery came up and unlimbered, but one gun couldn't fire till our wounded were removed, as otherwise it would have run on to them during the recoil. There was a fair amount of shell-fire; some struck short, but most of them fell about thirty yards behind us. The Chinese evidently had the range of the embankment. All their shells appeared to be common shell with percussion fuse. Our guns fired indirect fire, aligned on iron rods driven into the top of the bund for some time. Then they limbered up and moved on ahead, and we were ordered to follow. The regiments in front of us - the 24$^{th}$ P.I. and 1$^{st}$ Sikhs - advanced through the crops to the north on the villages there in succession.

At 6 A.M. the chief of the staff - General Barrow - ordered us to advance to the attack on the left of the Sikhs. Captain Bingley started with his double company, and ten minutes later we followed with the next one. I told Captain Robin to take his double company still farther to the left and advance, covering our left outer flank. The 23$^{rd}$ Royal Welsh Fusiliers advanced in support of us; the crops were very high, but we could see our shrapnel bursting over the villages in front, one of which was in flames, and towards which we advanced, through intense heat and crops about ten feet high. We could not hear the enemy's bullets owing to the rustling made by our progress through the crops, but in the patches of open ground we heard them patting on the ground, and the soil jumping, and so many struck in one place, that though I had a sprained ankle I thought it advisable to dismount.

After moving some distance, the troops lost touch, and I found myself alone with about fifty men of the regiment. Captain Jermyn, D.A.A.G.,* 1$^{st}$ Brigade, now galloped up and told us to move more to the left to clear the line of fire of our battery, which was going to re-open fire. We did so, and

* Deputy Assistant Adjutant General. See page 46

51

*Squadron, 16th Bengal Lancers. A unit of this regiment took part i.*

*f of the Legations, but it is uncertain where this photograph was taken.*

crossed some open ground, and then some Chinese trenches cleverly screened with straw, and came on three or four companies of Japanese in close order with two field guns. Their officer rode up, and by signs gave us to understand that our guns had killed some of their men. I gave him a note saying so, and moved up on the Japanese right. Bullets were falling thick here, and I saw some of the 1$^{st}$ Sikhs lying down on my right, and moved up to them. Several shells were bursting just in front of and behind us, while we were in a small clearing.

We now moved to the right, reached a road, and halted. The Sikhs also had lost the rest of their regiment. After a rest and a look round with some scouts to see where we were, we returned to the road and marched up it with the Sikhs and a Japanese regiment, and found the rest of our force, after going about half a mile. The Japanese cavalry and 1$^{st}$ Bengal Lancers had been on our left outer flank the whole time, but we didn't know this until we saw their lances over the high crops, just before we met the Japanese column with two guns. Heat now became terrific; after a halt, we crossed the Pei-ho River by a bridge of boats, together with the rest of our force; threw out outposts, sent out reconnoitering parties, and bivouacked.

Let us see what despatches say. "As arranged, in the early hours of the 5$^{th}$ inst., the turning movement commenced. At daybreak the column came under a heavy fire from the right front, and the action began with a vigorous forward movement of the Japanese against the entrenchments, supported on the right by the British. The brunt of the action fell on the Japanese, who attacked and stormed line after line in the most gallant manner. Our troops, in consequence of their position, scarcely fired a shot, and I readily accord to the Japanese the whole credit of the victory. Their loss was, I understand, about three hundred killed and wounded, while ours was only twenty-five. The Chinese rout was complete, and before noon they had entirely disappeared, having fled to the left bank of the river. The other allied forces were scarcely engaged at all, and practically had no loss. After the victory at Pei-tsang, we pushed on for a mile or two along the right bank, but being stopped by inundations, were compelled to return to Pei-tsang, and cross over to the left bank, where we bivouacked for the night, covered by a strong outpost two or three miles in advance."

The 1$^{st}$ Sikhs went on a reconnaissance, and the 1$^{st}$ Bengal Lancers, when reconnoitering, fired on some Russians by mistake, and were fired at in return. Explanations were given, and the Russian commander, on being informed that one Lancer was wounded, replied, "I also have one man wounded. It is all right; we are quits." A small defensive post was formed here, consisting of British, Americans, and Japanese. Lieutenant Meadows, Subadar Gujraj Singh, and fifty rifles of the 7$^{th}$ Rajputs, formed the British portion. I went to General Stewart's camp that evening, where the situation was explained, and orders were issued for the next day.

On August 6$^{th}$ we rose and marched early. Owing to the bad state of the road, the naval 12-pounders had to be placed in junks, and towed up the river as far as Tung-chow, from which place they reached Pekin by road. After going some distance we met a large force of Russians moving by another road on our left, probably that along the river bank. Captain Jermyn, D.A.A.G., rode up and said, "The General's orders are for you to halt and allow the Russians to pass (cross, he said, as well as I can remember) our line of march." The Russians, however, instead of crossing, followed on the same route, and were succeeded by the French. They took one hour to pass, and then piled arms, blocking the road. We were thus separated from the head of the column. However, we moved on, and leaving the French and Russians to follow the short main road, took the more circuitous track along the river bank, and in this way recovered much lost ground, and halted at a village on the river bank. Suddenly guns began firing to our front, and we could see smoke rising in clouds at a distance estimated to be about three or four miles away. The road being still blocked, we struck across the fields, and by dint of hard marching across country towards the sound of the guns, at length reached a village, where we could see where the staff were, by two long ladders fixed upright and locked together perched on a mound, with men standing on them. As the whole of our staff appeared to be there, I left the regiment, galloped forward, and was met by Captain Pell, A.D.C.* He said: "The orders are for you to double up your men and advance in extended order. The Americans are on your right, and the Russians on your left. You will come under shell fire about 400 yards farther on."

I turned and signalled the regiment to join me, and as they arrived, formed them up in quarter column behind the brow of the hill. Magazines were charged. The men badly required a short rest before going into action, as they were already dead beat, every one of them. The heat was now 105 degrees in the shade, but the situation would admit of no delay. General Gaselee ordered us to advance on a village ahead, over which we could see our shrapnel bursting. Captain Bingley was told to extend his companies to form our right, and Captain Robin our left; our left being on the road leading to the village, and our right near the railway line.

As we advanced, we saw two of our Maxims on the top of the railway embankment blazing away to the north-west, and we passed a battery of English and Russian guns in action on our left. A shell burst occasionally here and there, and we passed a lot of wounded being brought back, and men exhausted by the heat were lying about. Our advance was consequently very slow, as many of our men could hardly

* Aide-de-Camp. See page 45

move owing to the heat and want of water. When we reached the village the firing had ceased; it was all over. We then formed up in the shade, and waited for orders, and drank muddy water. After resting about half-an-hour, the Russian Infantry came up and marched on without halting. One of their men fell down as they were passing us, evidently overcome by the heat, and our doctor, Captain Walton, I.M.S.,* went to his assistance, and taking a cap from off a Russian soldier's head, began fanning the prostrate man, and looked after him till the Russian medical officer arrived.

Although the 7$^{th}$ Rajputs were in rear during this fight, and although I was not an eye-witness of what occurred, yet I think the following account taken from the despatches, and from the descriptions of those actually present, will be of interest.

The allied forces marched by the right bank of the river with the exception of about 6000 Japanese, who continued to advance by the left bank. The British troops were leading when Yang-tsun was sighted, the Russians and French as already described following them. The American troops were on the right flank. The enemy's main position was apparently along the railway embankment, with one flank resting on a village close to the Pei-ho railway bridge. The troops advanced in the following order:-

American troops, the 14$^{th}$ Infantry, on the right; British in the centre; and Russian Infantry on the left. On the extreme right were the 1$^{st}$ Bengal Lancers; the 1$^{st}$ Sikhs formed the first line of the British troops; the 23$^{rd}$ Royal Welsh Fusiliers and the 24$^{th}$ Punjab Infantry formed the second line. The artillery of the British force took up a position to the left; whence they covered the advance, and where they were joined by a Russian

* Indian Medical Service

57

battery later on. The American guns were to the right of the railway; the advance was rapidly conducted over the level plain, the distance traversed being about 5000 yards. The ground was covered with high crops, but not quite so thickly as at Pei-tsang. After passing rather more than half this distance, the troops came under a hot shell and musketry fire, but owing to the open order in which the British force worked, their losses were comparatively slight. During the advance, owing to the nature of the ground, the front gradually narrowed, and the British and American lines overlapped. When close to the position the order to cease fire was given, and as soon as the Russians on the left stopped firing, the order to charge was given, and the Sikhs and Americans charged, the men of both forces being mixed up together. The $24^{th}$ Punjab Infantry were in the second line, which was formed of three extended lines fifty yards behind each other, and the first of these three lines was up in time to join in the charge on the left of the $1^{st}$ Sikhs. The Welsh Fusiliers, owing to the conformation of the ground, were rather wedged out of the assaulting line.

The Chinese held the villages on the left, south side of the railway, until the troops charged. The troops on the right carried the railway embankment, and those on the left cleared the villages. As the Chinese ran, they turned and fired at our troops, who were clearing the first village. Then they fled over the embankment, and their guns being in a retired position escaped capture. The fight was now practically ended, and the troops rallied and formed up near the second village, and under cover of the railway embankment.

The following officers were mentioned in despatches as having specially distinguished themselves :

Major T. E. Scott, D.S.O., $1^{st}$ Sikh Infantry.
Lieut. W. F. Bainbridge (Adjutant), $1^{st}$ Sikh Infantry.
Captain J. H. Gwyne, Royal Welsh Fusiliers.

The names of the following American officers were also mentioned for the same reason:-

Major W. Quinton, and Captain J. R. M. Taylor, 14$^{th}$ U.S. Infantry.

No. 4995, Private Jackson, Royal Welsh Fusiliers, was also mentioned for the following act:-

"Some shells from one of the batteries engaged were taking our troops and the Americans in reverse. Private Jackson volunteered to get up on the embankment, and tried to communicate with the battery, and while doing so, was exposed to fire from both sides."

The 2$^{nd}$ battalion Royal Welsh Fusiliers had two killed and eight wounded. The Sikhs had five men killed; one British officer and nineteen men wounded. The 24$^{th}$ Punjab Infantry one man killed and ten wounded.

It was during this action that an unfortunate incident occurred. The British field battery had taken up its position, and were shelling the enemy, when a Russian battery came up on their left and got into action. The Russian officers took the range from the British battery, but owing to some mistake, our gun sights being sighted in yards and theirs in metres, they fired short, and several of their shells exploded amongst the 1$^{st}$ Sikhs and U.S. Infantry, who were advancing in attack formation against the Chinese position, killing several men. Firing over the heads of advancing infantry during the attack and up to the last moment is excellent, but when, as in this case, the troops are advancing through high crops, and the guns, owing to the flatness of the country, have but little command of view, accidents are always likely to happen. Most soldiers would prefer to take the risk of advancing during the last few hundred yards without the aid of their own guns, the enemy thereby

*ery*

gaining an advantage for this short period, than face the possibility of being shot by their own side.

While halted here and waiting for orders, I climbed up on to the lofty railway embankment close by, and stood on the site of the station, which had been utterly destroyed by the Boxers; even the very foundations of the houses had been dug up. Our field battery now came up, and from this elevated position opened fire on the villages through which the enemy were retreating. Many dead Chinamen lay about. Close by was the railway bridge over the Pei-ho, an iron girder bridge supported on concrete piers. The Boxers had partially destroyed the pier on the farther bank, and the girder was still resting on the piers, but so displaced that trains could not cross it. Had they completely destroyed the bridge piers, letting the girders fall into the water, it is difficult to see how the boat column could have continued its advance until the removal of the obstacle, which would have taken some time. The railway embankment and the culverts were standing, but rails, sleepers, rolling-stock and tanks were destroyed.

Orders soon came to bivouac, and the men were told off to it, a simple process. The staff show you your frontage, and tell you how deep your bit of ground is, while you set to work and make the best of it. This time it happened to be crops. The regiment is marched up, and each company piles arms on the site allotted to it. The positions for the hospital, transport, and quarter-guard are indicated, and the officers' bivouac; and sentries are posted. Then off into the nearest village we go to lay hold of anything in the way of a bit of matting, a blanket, or a door that will afford some shelter from the piercing rays of the sun. In about an hour's time we are all more or less sheltered; the officers under a "lean-to" of matting, and the doctor "babu,"* the hospital assistant or native apothecary, is

* An Indian (usually a clerk) able to write English.

sitting in a shelter made for him by his Kahars*, a structure of long maize stalks plaited together, the roots being in the ground, and a roof of poles thatched with large green leaves. A Sepoy has twisted some maize stalks together, spread his coat on the top, and is happy. There is a stir and commotion in the next camp; men running and tumbling over each other, and from the midst of them a hare escapes and rushes into our territory, where he is collared, and appears later on in the mess kettle.

On August 7$^{th}$ we halted to allow supplies to be brought up. The boat column arrived, mooring near the camp, and we were able to indulge in the luxury of a wash and change of clothes. The Pei-ho water, however, is so muddy that it is almost like pea-soup, and after drying one's self, the towels appeared as if made of khaki-coloured material.

* Carriers.

# CHAPTER III.

## UNDER HOT SKIES

The sights one saw during the advance were curious. One day we passed a long train of Russian baggage. The officer of the baggage escort was sitting in a rickshaw and driving a mule which he had ingeniously harnessed into the vehicle in the place of the ordinary coolie. On another occasion we passed a quantity of abandoned Chinese umbrellas lying strewn along the road, where they had evidently been left by the Chinese troops in their hasty flight. As the sun was very hot at the time the men picked them up as they passed, and opening them, held them over their heads, when the column presented the curious sight of a mass of troops moving with umbrellas; but not for long, for though shady, they gave extra weight to carry, and were soon thrown away. One officer, however, wiser than the rest, retained a couple, and regularly bivouacked under them for the rest of the march. My old bearer managed to secure a cart and a mule and drove along in triumph, but not for long. The cart and mule were claimed and taken by their rightful owner the next day, but we managed to secure another mule, which we kept for the rest of the advance.

An interchange of accoutrements occasionally took place; foreign officers would be seen wearing our putties, and British officers wearing American gaiters, but this occurred more extensively after our arrival in Pekin, when kits and baggage had come up. Stowhasser gaiters, putties, and warm coats, British, were in great demand by the German officers, also our riding-breeches; while American gauntlets, both fur-lined and unlined, were eagerly sought after by the Britisher, as was the American head-gear for wear in quarters. If a committee on clothing had sat in Pekin during the occupation, by taking one article of kit from one nation and another from another, they would probably have evolved the most perfect dress and equipment for a soldier that the world has yet seen, for each equipment had some good point in which it excelled the others.

On some of the hottest days during the advance, we passed numbers of soldiers of other nations who had fallen out owing to fatigue or sunstroke. Most of those we observed were Americans and Japanese, the troops who were ahead of us. Whenever the Japs fell out, they collected together and formed small parties, who bivouacked along the side of the road, the men taking off their accoutrements, piling arms, and cooking. When rested, they moved on again. The Americans acted in much the same manner; in places the roads were strewn with articles of soldiers' equipment, haversacks, great-coats and blankets which, in the terrific heat which prevailed, the men found themselves unable to carry. Occasionally an American cart, looking something like a waggonette with an awning, and drawn by four mules, would come down the road from the front to pick up stray pieces. At one point we marched through an American detachment; the men were marching slowly along at about two miles an hour, with heads bent and eyes half closed, as though sleeping or dead tired, and though utterly knocked up by the heat, yet determined to stick to it and come into camp on their own feet. I don't think they even noticed us as we passed them.

We used to spread out on the march as much as possible, as a rule taking the two edges of the road and the narrow smooth track in the middle. If one looked back from the head of the column, one could only see for about twenty yards; the rest was a cloud of dust. The signal to halt was a whistle blown and a hand held up over the head. The men then halted, and without any word of command sat down on the sides of the road. A blast on the whistle and a wave of the hand set them in motion again. This was the usual procedure, but in the vicinity of the enemy the men were kept closed up and lookouts were posted. The men wore their coats unbuttoned at the neck, their shoulders and the lower parts of their pugarees* being black with sweat. Putties were worn as the wearer preferred, usually inside the boot to prevent its chafing above the ankle. Shoes in lieu of boots, if a man had them, were worn. Water-carriers (bhisties) marched alongside each company with two empty kerosene tins, one at each end of a pole, over their shoulders. These they filled at the various wells we passed, while the water-mules with their water-tanks followed close in rear of the regiment.

Water to a man marching in a hot sun is as fuel to an engine, neither can get along without it. Many times I saw men who were done up and unable to proceed, after drinking water and bathing their faces get up and march on. All boots were greased or oiled after landing in China, and blacking, whose chief use is show, was discarded.

On August 8$^{th}$ we resumed the march, and passed through several lines of Chinese entrenchments all abandoned. A few dead bodies were lying about. We then crossed the Pei-ho by the bridge of boats, and found the place crowded with Japanese troops. As we entered one village we saw the head of a Chinaman hanging by the pigtail from a post by the road-side. The field telegraph was laid as we went, and surveyors were busy surveying the route. The heat, as usual, was excessive, and very oppressive, owing to the crops, about ten feet high, which prevented any circulation of the air.

On the 9th we advanced to Hoshiwu, a long, tedious, and dusty march, without a breath of air stirring, as usual. As we drew near the village we saw a number of Chinese standards

* Usually a thin scarf, probably worn as a form of light turban.

guarded by sowars* of the 1<sup>st</sup> Bengal Lancers. Two squadrons of these, under Major Hayes and Lieutenant Sproule, with Lieutenant Keeble, M.I., as interpreter, were ordered to form part of a mixed force, with one squadron Japanese cavalry and one sotnia** Cossacks, the whole under command of a Japanese colonel.

The squadrons 1<sup>st</sup> B.L. left camp at 3 A.M. on the 9<sup>th</sup>, and joined the rest of the force, which had bivouacked in advance, at daybreak, when orders were issued as follows:-

"The enemy is supposed to be in force at Hoshiwu. The Japanese division will attack him. The cavalry force will cover the left flank."

The force moved off through densely cultivated country, in line, covered by advanced patrols. About 11 A.M. a high embankment stretching right across the country was encountered. The 1<sup>st</sup> B.L. halted on the farther side of this, and the rest of the cavalry on the near side. The country ahead was flat and covered with high crops, villages being dotted about. After about half-an-hour a few mounted men were seen to issue from a village about a mile farther on; these were soon followed by many armed men on foot. It was decided to advance on them.

The Japanese squadron, with the two squadrons 1<sup>st</sup> B.L., trotted towards the village. One troop 1<sup>st</sup> B.L., under Jemadar*** Khuda Baksh Khan, covered the advance of the Indian cavalry. As the main body neared the village heavy firing was heard, and scouts from the Jemadar brought back word that he was being hard pressed on the farther side. Upon this the two squadrons broke into a gallop, and moved round the village to the right. Nothing was seen at first except the

* Indian Army term for troopers in the Lancer Regiments.
** A unit of Cossack cavalry, roughly equivalent to a squadron.
*** Indian rank equivalent to Second Lieutenant.

Japanese, who had dismounted and were firing on the village, while the enemy were running about in all directions. When our force had cleared the trees, which were thick near the village, a number of tall standards came in sight, and gave a point for attack, which was at once taken advantage of. The enemy made but feeble resistance. In a couple of minutes they were dispersed, and fled in all directions.

In their flight they passed through another large village full of armed men, who opened a weak fire on the Indian squadrons. This also was cleared, and the enemy completely scattered, many men and horses being killed, and various standards captured.

As it was unknown what further forces might be at hand, and as the horses were exhausted, the rally was sounded.

The force of the enemy probably consisted of about 250 horsemen and a number of men on foot. The dead principally wore the uniform of Chinese regular troops, and were armed with magazine rifles and carbines*. Our force was about 150 Indian and 80 Japanese cavalry. Our casualties - two horses killed, and two men slightly wounded.

After resting, the force proceeded without further incident to Hoshiwu, a Japanese infantry battalion which meantime had come up clearing off the enemy's infantry, with some little loss to themselves.

The Chinese cavalry were, I hear, utterly demoralised after this, and the sight of a few lance-heads appearing over the crops was always sufficient to make them clear out.

The enemy had apparently intended to make a stand at Hoshiwu, as the village there was loopholed** and partly

* Carbines were short barrelled, lightweight rifles mainly used (in European armies) by the cavalry.
** See footnote on page 76.

69

entrenched, the crops in front of it having been cut low to afford a field of fire; but our rapid movements upset his calculations.

The Chinese had made an immense cutting at this place, intending to inundate the country on our line of advance, and lower the level of the river, so that it would be impossible for our boats to get up, thus stopping our advance. We found the cutting nearly completed, and the workmen's tools and baskets lying in it, so precipitately had they fled. However, although the thing didn't come off, the Chinese general informed his government that he had cut the banks of the Pei-ho, and inundated the country, drowning 25,000 of the foreigners, at which, he naively concluded, "they are much disheartened." We read this account of our being drowned some months later in a Chinese paper, and were much amused.

The boat column came up that evening and moored by our bivouac, and we enjoyed a bathe. The river was about three feet six inches deep in the deepest part, with a very strong current and sandy bottom, and so swift that one couldn't walk up stream against it. The troops had been much exhausted during the day's march, and we passed numbers of Japanese and American troops overcome by the heat. Many of the British fell out too, and groups of men were seen lying by the roadside in places. Blankets and accoutrements were passed lying here and there, and several men were lying apparently senseless, and were twitching their legs. However, the Europeans stuck to it pluckily till they could hold on no longer, and even Sepoys fell out overcome by the heat. The universal cry was "Water, water." The cavalry, as well as the artillery, lost several horses that day, simply from the heat.

It fell to the lot of the British force to march the next day by night. We accordingly started in the afternoon, the men cheering as they left camp, according to their custom. After clearing the village we passed a French force bivouacked among some trees on our left. This was one of the only two occasions during the advance on Pekin on which I saw French troops; the other was on the morning of the sixth, before Yang-tsun, when they were following in rear of the Russian army. The Russians, or at any rate a portion of them, arrived on the scene of battle; the French did not. The French troops present during the advance, unlike other regiments of the French contingent, were of puny stature and inferior physique. They were marines, I believe, from Tonkin, and were apparently unable to keep up with the rest of the allies; otherwise it is difficult to account for their absence on every important occasion.

The third occasion on which they were seen was on the afternoon of the 15$^{th}$ August, when they arrived at the carriage park near the Legations, just twenty-four hours after the Indian troops, so much decried by French officers and journalists, had relieved them.

We were comfortably going along when suddenly a penetrating crack appeared to rend the air. My horse staggered, everybody halted and instinctively looked round to where we saw an immense flame shoot up into the sky. Then, after a lapse of some seconds a tremendous booming report reached us; a cloud of dark smoke appeared high up in the air like a ball, full of convolutions all in motion. These kept shooting and rolling out while the cloud continued spreading and spreading until it appeared to cover half the sky. Then, in a minute or two, tiny little black threads appeared to rain from the sky on to us. We must have been about three miles from the place when the explosion occurred. This was the blowing up of the Chinese powder magazine at Hoshiwu, which was exploded by us one hour after the column had left. The men cheered and we resumed the march at about midnight, the moon being full and well up.

We passed through several villages and a small town. The houses had been turned out already, chairs and tables at which we sat when halted were in the streets, and corpses lying in the pale light presented a weird sight. After what seemed an interminable march, we were pointed out the direction of our bivouac, and the river bank looming in the distance; but moonlight, modified by a haze from the river, is very deceptive. As Longfellow aptly says, "Things are not what they seem,"* and they weren't on this occasion. However, in a flat country one bit of ground full of high crops is just as good a bivouac as another, so we lay down where we were, and moved on a few hundred yards to the river bank in the morning.

This place was called Matao, and our halting-place was covered with Indian corn, which was ready for eating. A good deal of diarrhoea was prevalent during the advance, even those who drank nothing but tea and filtered water suffering from it, but I expect eating unripe melons and other fruit was responsible for much of it. We left Matao on the afternoon of August 11th, reached Changchowan in the night, and halted, finding the ground cold and damp from the wet stalks of the crops we lay down in. The officers bivouacked by some graves. At dawn we saw the dead body of a Boxer lying close by on his face; he had seven sword or bayonet thrusts in his back, but no bullet wound that I could see. The usual Boxer sign of a red sash was on him.

As we were having a light meal about eight o'clock, the sun already being unpleasantly hot, the order came that we were to march in an hour's time; so off we went. It was a short march, and before long we arrived at Tung-chou and halted there, piling arms on the river side where there was an open piece of ground. Men were now allowed to fall out and rest in

* From *A Psalm of Life.*

the shade of the buildings lining the river front, while we officers went into a deserted house close by, telling off as many men as they would hold to the rooms we had not reserved for ourselves.

Tung-chou, a town about fifteen miles from Pekin, with which it is connected by several roads and a canal, is the point at which passengers and goods coming up by river land for that city. It was early in June that the mission buildings at this place were looted and burnt. The missionaries fled and escaped with their lives, but seventy-five of their less fortunate converts were massacred, some of them being burnt alive.

When we arrived the cavalry had already been through the place, but we managed to make ourselves fairly comfortable all the same, and sat down that day, for the first time during the advance, at a table with cushioned chairs. In the evening we bathed in the river; the water was very shallow, and one had to go out about sixty yards to get it over one's waist. During the day there were some shots fired by the Bengal Lancers' vedettes*, who were out on the farther bank, and some captures were made of prisoners and boats laden with arms and ammunition coming down a side stream.

In the evening I was summoned to headquarters, and there, sitting out on the roof top, the General described the plan of campaign that was intended for the following days. The first day reconnaissances were to be sent out towards Pekin; on the second day the troops would concentrate, and on the third Pekin would be attacked. What immediately concerned us, however, was that the $7^{th}$ Rajputs were to proceed on a reconnaissance towards Pekin at dawn next day, the force to consist of $1^{st}$ Bengal Lancers, $7^{th}$ Rajputs, and two guns of the $12^{th}$ Field Battery Royal Artillery. The enemy was supposed to

* Mounted sentries at or in advance of outposts of an army or an encampment.

be concentrating somewhere to the south-south-east of the Chinese city, and our force would be on the left, the most exposed flank. Next to us on the right were the Americans, and then either the Russians or Japanese. We were to devote our special attention to a road or roads south of the canal, and the paved road from Tungchou to Pekin, and leading to the east gate of the Chinese city. This was, I believe, owing to information having been received from Sir Claude Macdonald that our easiest way into the Legations was *via* the Chinese city.

On the morning of the 13$^{th}$ we fell in and marched about an hour before dawn. We passed through a camp of Russian troops *en route*, and soon after reached the open country. There was great difficulty in working a cavalry screen* on such ground, for it was only when a man was close to you that you could tell his whereabouts by seeing the top of his lance - pennons were furled - above the high crops. The sun rose higher and higher, and it became intensely hot, so much so that many officers, feeling it even through their solah topees** (many wore what are known in India as Cawnpore tent club hats), thatched them inside with leaves of the maize, and the riders presented a curious appearance with the long green leaves showing from under their helmets, and hanging down nearly to their waist belts. The men of the 7$^{th}$ Rajputs had the ends of their pugarees undone and hanging loosely in folds over their faces or necks as a protection.

When we came to a village we halted, and the men fell out for water. These villages had not been disturbed except by our cavalry passing through, but nevertheless they were

* Usually a patrol of cavalrymen deployed so as to conceal (as far as possible) the movements of their accompanying infantry.

** Helmets, shaped rather like inverted pudding basins, made from spongy cellular tissue (pith) in the centre of plants.

completely deserted except by one or two old women and men who sat on stools in front of their doors in the main road, some blind, others crippled, but all evidently so old and worn out that they preferred to remain where they were and chance it, rather than obtain the certain death which the hardships of flying with the rest of their countrymen would involve.

After moving on as we calculated about eight miles, Colonel Gartside Tipping, who commanded the party, halted. A tomb enclosed by massive walls was close by, and there was water in the enclosure, so it was decided to rest here. Personally I was very glad, for just before we halted I had been touched up by the sun, and was just able to dismount and lie down, after drinking brandy and having cold water poured on my head; and after half-an-hour's rest in the shade, I was able to get up and go to the camping-ground and look round. The Colonel and I went there with a small escort; we found the caretakers ready to fly, but after showing that we meant no harm, they conducted us round and showed us the wells. The rest of the force was then sent for, and we bivouacked in the tomb. Sentries and vedettes were posted, and we settled down to rest. Messages occasionally came in by parties of troopers from the Americans, who were about one mile off on our right flank. Weak and tired after my touch of sun, I slept heavily during the night, and was awakened by somebody pulling my sleeve, and saying, "We are all to be ready to turn out at a moment's notice." I got up, put on my belts, and went out, and heard the sound of heavy firing, big guns, machine guns, and the rattle of musketry, which died away occasionally, and then revived. Messages came in from the vedettes saying they were fired on, and from the Americans saying that they expected to be attacked at any moment. We stood to arms; the line of defence was fixed on, trenches were thrown up, and every preparation made to meet an attack in force.

If any candidate at a garrison class examination had ever ventured to formulate such a scheme of defence, or take up the position we did and put it on paper, he would have been hopelessly spun in his exam. Nevertheless, I am convinced that what we did was the best that could possibly have been done under such circumstances, and was sound in the case in point. We were in a walled enclosure three times too large for our force. The walls were too thick to be loopholed,* and too high to be banquetted* for firing over the top; while if the wall had been suitable for either of these, it was surrounded on all sides by miles of crops ten or twelve feet high, into which you couldn't see for three yards. The crops were too green to burn; we had no cutting implements to clear them with, and if we had had, the men were far too exhausted by the hardships they had undergone since August 4$^{th}$ to do any more work. So it was decided to throw up trenches connecting the houses well in the inside of the enclosure, to hold them, and to open fire on the enemy as soon as he attempted to get over the enclosure wall, fifty to a hundred yards from our trenches. In the darkness we should have made a decided score, as they would have been visible against the sky-line, whilst we should have been in darkness; and the longest we could have had to hold out without relief was three or four hours. However, as dawn came the firing ceased. One of our men was reported missing during the night. It appears he, as customary with Hindus, had leisurely strolled out in the evening, taking his lotah** with him to perform his ablutions. Nothing was seen of him until next morning, when two sowars of the Bengal Lancers brought him in. It appears he had gone a short distance, and losing

* Loopholing is the creation of narrow vertical slits in a wall through which rifles could be aimed and fired: banquetting is the making of a raised footway behind a parapet or wall, on which soldiers may stand and (as Vaughan indicates) fire their rifles over the top.
** Brass pot

his way, wisely decided to remain where he was for the night, which he did, and the cavalry going out in the morning found him. He was well slated for his stupidity.

# Peking at the time of the Siege

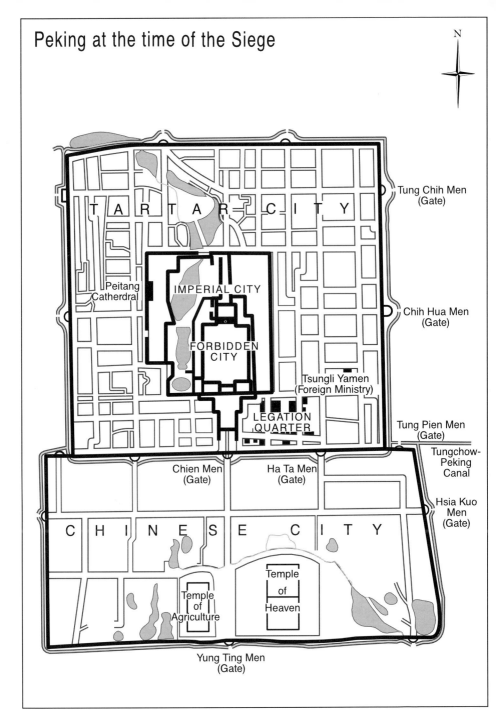

N

Tung Chih Men
(Gate)

T A R T A R C I T Y

Chih Hua Men
(Gate)

Peitang
Catherdral

IMPERIAL CITY

FORBIDDEN
CITY

Tsungli Yamen
(Foreign Ministry)

LEGATION
QUARTER

Tung Pien Men
(Gate)

Tungchow-
Peking
Canal

Chien Men
(Gate)

Ha Ta Men
(Gate)

Hsia Kuo
Men
(Gate)

C H I N E S E C I T Y

Temple
of
Heaven

Temple
of
Agriculture

Yung Ting Men
(Gate)

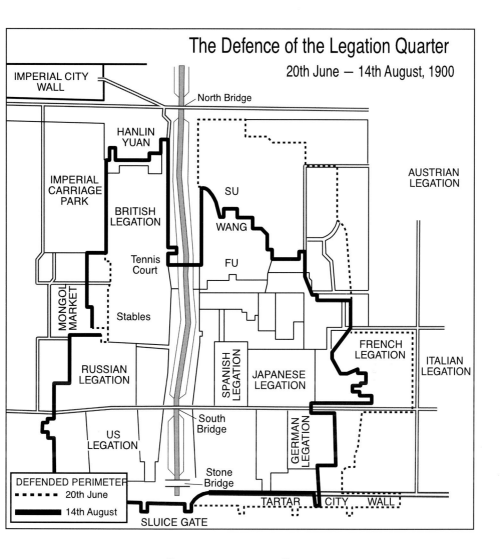

## The Defence of the Legation Quarter
### 20th June — 14th August, 1900

IMPERIAL CITY WALL

North Bridge

HANLIN YUAN

IMPERIAL CARRIAGE PARK

BRITISH LEGATION

SU

WANG

AUSTRIAN LEGATION

Tennis Court

FU

MONGOL MARKET

Stables

RUSSIAN LEGATION

SPANISH LEGATION

JAPANESE LEGATION

FRENCH LEGATION

ITALIAN LEGATION

South Bridge

US LEGATION

GERMAN LEGATION

Stone Bridge

DEFENDED PERIMETER
- - - - - 20th June
━━━━ 14th August

TARTAR CITY WALL

SLUICE GATE

The terms "Tartar City" and "Chinese City" used in the map of Peking on the opposite page derive from the Manchu capture of Peking in 1644 mentioned in the Editor's Foreword. The Chinese inhabitants of the area were then required to move out of that part of Peking which became known as the Tartar City and had to live in another walled area known as the South City or the Chinese City.

# COLOUR PLATES

80

# CHAPTER IV.

## IN THE DRAGON'S LAIR

On the fourteenth General Sir A. Gaselee with his staff arrived early in the morning and asked what the firing had been about. He had supposed on hearing it that we had been attacked, and consequently had left Tung-chou during the night with the rest of his force, and marched to our assistance. We told him what had happened, then ate a hurried breakfast, and received the order to get ready to march at once on Pekin. After we had advanced several miles the heat became excessive, and the General ordered a halt, during which he rode with his escort up a cross road to the north. For some reason or other, probably owing to a misapprehension on the part of the officer who conveyed us the order, we were ordered to follow, and finally arrived on a parallel road, where the American troops were. We then returned to the cross roads where we had first halted. The cavalry went to the front, and Lieutenant Vanderguch with one half company was sent up the road to reconnoitre.

Again we advanced, and when soon after a message was received from Lieutenant Vanderguch that the enemy were in position in a village on the right of the road, we were ordered to advance through the crops on that side; Captain Bingley with his double company on the left, his left on the road, one company extended and one in support. Captain Robin's double company in the same formation formed the right of the line. The other regiments, 1$^{st}$ Sikhs and 24$^{th}$ Punjab Infantry, were, I believe, advancing in a similar manner on the left of the road. After moving some distance, the guns opened fire down the road, and the shells came bursting over our heads. The advance was slow and tedious, owing to the high crops which everywhere obstructed the view. While advancing we saw a number of Chinese running through a village on our right flank, and a few volleys were fired at them by the right section of our line. Some of our cavalry now appeared in that direction, so that apparently these people were running away from them; anyhow, they disappeared. A few men seen crouching in the crops in front of us were shot.

Having arrived at the village, we were told to occupy it. There was a high castellated wall at the farther end, and the subadar-major* said: "I suppose we ought to occupy and hold the wall of that fort," pointing to it. I replied, "Yes," little knowing that it was the city wall of Pekin that we were in sight of. We halted there for some time, heavy firing going on amongst the trees and villages on our right, where the Americans were.

While riding about collecting the men, many of whom had halted at the wells just before the village, I noticed that the wall appeared to be of great length, and concluded that it must be Pekin. As the companies closed they came into the village, and thence moved on to the city gate** close by. This gate when I arrived had been already captured. The 24$^{th}$ Punjab Infantry, who were on our left during the advance, reached the gate at the same time as a company of ours under Lieutenant Loch. This officer then went back to inform our battery that the infantry had reached the city walls. The gate was barred, and there were no means of opening it. No enemy was seen by the party at the gate, though men's heads were visible at the embrasures*** in the walls to the right of it farther off. These were fired at and disappeared. Sepoy Janes ha Singh, 22$^{nd}$

* Senior Indian Officer.   ** The Hsia Kuo Men
*** (In military use) Opening in a wall or parapet, widening from within, through which guns might be fired.

Punjab Infantry, attached to the 24$^{th}$, climbed up in an angle formed by the wall, and letting down his pugaree, assisted Major Climo and some men of the 24$^{th}$ on to the wall. Another party climbed the wall a little farther south. These then descended inside the walls of the city, and opened the two gates to the troops. Shortly after General Sir A. Gaselee arrived, and Captain Keyes, R.N., hoisted the white ensign over the gate.

Two one-pounder quick-firing Krupp guns were found by the 24$^{th}$ on the walls by the gate. As we marched through the gate there was some shooting going on, which I concluded was our troops on the city walls firing down into the town. We advanced for about half a mile to an open space, where the General and staff were, the place being picketed by a company of ours under Subadar Adhar Singh, who had pushed on to this point after the city gates were opened. Here we halted to allow the rear of the regiment to come up. Everybody, both officers and men, were much exhausted with the long advance through the crops. General Barrow showed me a map of Pekin, and pointed out the position of the Legations and the line of advance of our main body. Our regiment was to advance independently, covering the right flank, and work towards the sluice gate. A naval officer who knew Pekin then explained to me the position and appearance of the gate. I asked whether if we arrived at the Legations we should enter, and the General said, "Yes, if you can."

Off we started, one company on our right flank as a flank guard, and a few men a little way ahead of the main body as an advanced guard. Shells were bursting with good effect on the south-east corner of the Tartar city, bringing down masses of masonry and raising clouds of dust. On we went, moving always westward, and every now and then taking a turn to the right northwards, but not moving too far in that direction, so as to avoid coming under fire from the walls of the Tartar city. The rattle of musketry appeared to come from all directions, and bullets were striking the dusty road, the walls, and roofs of the houses. As we worked northwards the flank guard got into the same road, and became part of our column. We kept as much as possible on the south sides of the streets to get shade. Not a Chinaman was to be seen, but the banging of doors was heard, and many of the rings hanging from the door knobs were shaking as we passed, showing that the doors had only just been shut. At last we entered a long and broad street, and while going up it saw hundreds of Chinamen running down the side streets away from us. As they were within one hundred and fifty yards, a glance showed that they were unarmed, so they were not fired at.

After going some distance we halted on the shady side of the road, and bullets began to fly down it, coming from our rear. Some one said, "Look out, the Sikhs are firing on our rearguard." I saw the rearguard extended across the road and firing at the Chinese. The Sikhs were at this time working towards the Chienmen Gate by another route, and were separated from us by several rows of houses. The doors of many of them were open, and I went into one close by, a china shop. Everything was there complete except the owner, who must have just bolted. The sentries posted during the halt being very close, I called to two men to follow, intending to put them out further ahead of us. To do so I rode across a road, at the north end of which was a gate of the Tartar city, Hatamen Gate. As I did so, I heard a tick-tick, as if some one was tapping the scaffolding poles, of which there were a number bunched together by the roadside, with a hammer. This happened again on my return, and I looked carefully up and down the street, but could not tell whence the bullets were coming from, so deceptive is smokeless powder. Suddenly my eye caught a puff of smoke coming from the rampart of the gateway, and heads were seen appearing and disappearing at the embrasures. A section or more of men were called up and ordered to fire with fixed sights at the embrasures and windows of the gateway. We supposed the distance to be nearly six hundred yards, but actual measurement afterwards proved it to be four hundred and fifty only.

*7th Rajputs at the Hatamen Gate, August 14th 1900*

After a while the firing from the gateway seemed to slacken, and we continued the advance northwards, up a side street parallel to the Hatamen Road, but west of it, keeping well up on the east side, so that the houses sheltered us partly from the gate. Captain Parr pointed out a narrow lane running west, which we took. Only one man could pass at a time, so a few men ran along it to the further end, and on their signalling " all clear" we advanced. As we moved on, an officer reported that the men were very tired in rear, and could not keep up, so they were told to remain halted, and follow on as soon as rested by the same route as we went, and that we were going to press on to the Legations. The party that went on were Lieutenant Loch,

85

myself, about thirty Sepoys, and one or two native officers. The streets from this point onwards were entirely deserted. The men were told by Loch that our object in thus pressing on was to relieve the Legations as soon as possible, and be the first regiment to enter. Tired and exhausted as they were, they began to run in their excitement, and I had to check them, as it was taking too much out of them.

After going some distance further along the road, we met General Gaselee and staff, with his escort of the 1$^{st}$ Sikhs, coming up a cross road. General Barrow said, "Yes, that's all right," meaning that we had hit off the line of advance intended for us. We followed them for a few yards, and came out on an open piece of ground which looked down on the ditch; the walls of the Tartar city were in front of us, but there was no one on them. The inner tower of the Hatamen Gate now began to fire on us (it was the outer gate that had fired while we were crossing the road), and some one said, "We shall have to take that gate." General Gaselee then ordered us to go on down along the road to the west, *i.e.* to continue on in our original direction. We went on, the men keeping close under the houses on the north side of the street to cover them from fire from the city walls and from the fire from the Hatamen Gate. We were now in a street separated by one row of houses only from the ditch and walls of the city; the whole place was completely deserted. At last an opening appeared in the houses on our right, and we saw the English, American, and other European flags hanging idly in folds from the flagstaffs erected on the bastions of the walls, for not a breath of air was stirring.

Our first impression was - well, all the Powers have managed somehow to get into the city before us, and we felt annoyed. Then we saw a head or two appear over the battlements, and a sailor standing right up on the wall waving a signal flag. Then the low roof of the sluice gate arch appeared, and the sailor lowered his flag and waved it towards it; we followed the track down into the ditch, which was flanked by the works of the Hatamen and Chien-men Gates. The whole space was clear. I turned to Loch and said, "Why, I believe these are the Legations." I shouted to the sailor, "Which way?" and he pointed again; then more heads cautiously appeared, hats were waved, and the people on the ramparts began to cheer, to which we responded, and so amid the cheering we entered the cutting joining the sluice gate to the ditch, and reaching the gate halted.

The gate was heavily barred, and through it we could see another similarly barred, and an American guard coming down with rifles in their hands. The Americans cut out a bar from each of the gates, and we entered one by one through the narrow opening thus made. We went up the ditch and climbed up the bank, or rather were hauled up by the crowds of Chinese Christians that met us, and we sat down in the shade by the side of the bridge in Legation Street. Europeans came rushing up waving hats and hand-shaking. We loosened our belts and made ourselves comfortable. After a brief interval, General Gaselee and his party came up out of the ditch, and we stood up and saluted. Immediately after a well-dressed man in mufti* came round the corner and shook hands with the General. This was Sir Claude Macdonald. Both then went on together.

After we had sat there some time a young lady without a hat and carrying a fan in her hand offered to show us the way to the British Legation, where we could get water, which all wanted badly. So we were led through the Russian Legation, a sentry there saying, "You English? very good," as we passed him. We passed a cemetery and a girls' school, who cheered us, and reached the lawn in front of the British Legation, where we piled arms. The whole place was crowded with Europeans,

* Civilian clothing

*The Sluice Gate*

cheering and waving their hats, and perfectly indifferent to the hail of bullets which were pattering against the roofs and upper parts of the walls around them.

We lay down and rested ourselves, but only for a short time, as we were soon ordered to the Japanese Legation. We went there by a covered way, crossing the sluice gate ditch. The Japanese officer, Colonel Shiba, was very polite, but said that he didn't want any reinforcements. I told him we were very tired, and would like to rest there if he didn't mind; so the men sat outside in the shade while I went in and talked to him, and had tea, pegs,* sandwiches, &c., which were most acceptable. After resting a little time we returned to the British Legation. By this time the rest of the regiment had arrived, and we piled arms on the lawn in front of the Legation.

To return to the rest of the troops. The point where the chief of the staff gave us our orders was also the point where the other regiments closed up and received theirs. After the 24th Punjab Infantry had entered the city, the man previously referred to as the first to climb over the city wall caught a Chinese pony and mounted it. For some reason or other he lost control of the animal, which bolted, and took him straight away towards the enemy. This man was never seen again alive.

The 24th Punjab Infantry were ordered to march to the Temple of Heaven, situated in the southern portion of the Chinese city, and secure its enclosures as a camping-ground for the troops. Major Parsons, interpreter to the 1st Brigade, undertook to show the way. As they passed through the streets, accompanied by a small body of the 1st Bengal Lancers, a few shots were fired at them from the houses; but the temple was soon occupied, those inside the enclosure offering no serious opposition.

* Alcoholic refreshment!

Later in the day four guns of the Field Battery arrived and opened fire on the south gate of the city, which was still held by the Chinese, and a company of the 24$^{th}$ was sent to cut off the enemy's retreat towards the east. The fire of the guns drove the Chinese out of the gatehouse, and many were killed and wounded by shell fire as they fled westward along the city walls. The main body, consisting of the General and staff with two guns of the Field Battery, the 23$^{rd}$ Royal Welsh Fusiliers, the Hong Kong Maxim guns, and the 1$^{st}$ Sikhs proceeded along the road which runs due west through the Chinese city from the east to the west gates. On reaching what was judged to be a point nearly south of the sluice gate, the Lieutenant-General with his staff and an escort of a company and a half of the 1$^{st}$ Sikhs under Major Scott branched off to the north to endeavour to reach it, while the remainder of the column, under General Sir Norman Stewart, continued their advance to the west up to the Chien-men Gate. The gate was closed, and the Chinese opened fire on the column from the walls. This was replied to.

Now, to return to the besieged Legations. As soon as the defenders of the barricades on the Tartar city walls saw the relieving troops arriving, and heard the cheering, a party of the Legation Guards, headed by Mr. Squires, charged out of their barricade and took the Chinese position close by them; then, keeping the Chinese on the run, they cleared the whole of the wall right up to the Chien-men Gate. Some of them then got down and opened one of the outer side gates. The Hong Kong Maxims, a party of the 1$^{st}$ Bengal Lancers under Lieutenant Macaulay, and the 1$^{st}$ Sikhs got through the gate, but were twice attacked while doing so. The enemy were so close that they actually laid hands on a carbine and a box of ammunition while the Maxim guns were being brought through. Lieutenant Bainbridge with a party of the 1$^{st}$ Sikhs hurried up on the west ramp of the Chien-men Gate and round on the outer wall, and cleared off the Chinese, who were firing at the column from the wall. This party also drove off the other Chinese attack, which was made from the direction of Legation Street, killing about fifty Chinese.

An immense number of Chinese from the direction of the Legations were now seen crossing the front - cavalry, infantry, and people in carts - all moving to the west, and on the route that runs past the south gate of the Imperial Palace by the Five Marble Bridges. The Maxims and infantry opened on these, the distance being about 800 yards, and men were seen falling in every direction. The column then proceeded down Legation Street, clearing the houses on both sides, and after scrambling over three barricades built across the street, entered the Russian Legation, and passed on through that to the British. General Stewart, with two guns and the Royal Welsh Fusiliers, proceeded along by the road under and outside of the walls of the Tartar city in an easterly direction from the Chien-men Gate, until he reached the sluice gate, which was entered. The guns were drawn up out of the ditch by hand up a ramp, and one of them, being taken across the bridge in Legation Street along the sides of which high walls were standing, was run out from the shelter of this and fired at two guns mounted on the walls of the Imperial city. Three shells were put into each embrasure, and the gun, which was under the enemy's musketry fire, withdrawn.

The small number of casualties that occurred during the entry into the city, considering the number of projectiles of all sorts that were flying about, was remarkable. The Chinese for the most part aimed badly and fired high; one feels bound, therefore, to place some credence in the prevalent rumour that the Chinaman thinks the higher he raises his back sight the greater the force with which the bullet will go.

With the men besieging the Legations, however, it was a different matter; they were said to have become excellent shots owing to constant practice, and any one exposing himself to view above a wall or through a loophole was pretty sure to be hit.

A sepoy of the 7$^{th}$ Rajputs, posted to a loophole in the redoubt covering the main entrance to the Legation, withdrew the brick in it, and was immediately struck in the face by a bullet. This occurred soon after our arrival.

The United States troops were on our right during the advance on Pekin. They advanced along the south bank of the Tung-chou Pekin Canal, and attacked the Tungpien-men or north-east gate of the Chinese city. It was their shells that we saw bursting with such good effect on the south-east corner tower of the Tartar city. The position of the gate they attacked was a very strong one. It was situated in a re-entering angle, and the advance of the attacking force was restricted to the space between the north wall of the Chinese city, and the canal was on a very narrow frontage. On reaching the outer of the two gates of the city, they found the Russians in possession of it, but making no attempt to go any further. They fired about twenty rounds at the inner gate, within a range of forty or fifty yards, and finally burst it open ; but on getting into the city they found that the direct line of their advance to the Legations was flanked the whole way by the Tartar city walls. The Americans here were engaged for about two hours in silencing the fire of the Chinese sharpshooters, who were stationed on the walls and on the tops of houses, and were extremely difficult to dislodge. The 14$^{th}$ Infantry and the Marines had six men wounded at this place. The troops then advanced along a street, removed by one or two rows of houses from the Tartar city walls, and parallel to it they passed the Hatamen Gate, and pressing on, entered the Legations by the sluice gate.

"On August 12$^{th}$ it was decided at a conference to send forward strong reconnoitring parties on the 13$^{th}$, to concentrate on a line about five miles from Pekin on the 14$^{th}$, and to attack on the 15$^{th}$. On the 14$^{th}$, however, owing to the premature advance of a battalion of one of the allied forces, the intended concentration was abandoned, and the troops all hurried forward to assault the city of Pekin." (Extract from despatches.)

The heavy fire heard during the night of the 13$^{th}$ was caused, according to camp rumour, by the Russians attacking that night. If they attacked prematurely in the hopes of stealing a march on their allies, and thereby increasing their prestige, they were disappointed. However, they conferred one benefit on us, which was unintended. As their attack went on hour after hour, the Chinese concluded that our main assault must be from that quarter, and the probability is that a large portion of their force was drawn away from the direction of the British advance to oppose them; otherwise, it seems difficult to account for the enemy holding the Chinese city so weakly.

The Legations had been relieved, the first troops to enter being the British under General Gaselee.

Thanks to the stimulus imparted to the leaders of the foreign troops by our Lieutenant-General, they had started in time. One shudders to think of what might have happened had they been too late. Sir Claude Macdonald, in his despatches referring to the night of August 13$^{th}$, says, "Three times during the night it was necessary to call up the reserves in support of the firing line, the attacks being more frequent than on any previous night." All certainly looks as if the Chinese in the city, aware of the approach of relief, had made a last effort to overwhelm the besieged.

It rained pretty hard during the night, and the lawn became uncomfortable, so I went into the shelter in front of the British Legation, packed full of guests and missionaries; a French priest, sitting up in his bed, pushed a cushioned chair towards me, in which I sat down and passed the rest of the night. Our officers lay on the lawn in front of the Legation for the night, while our men slept in the enclosure containing the Hanlin Library. The way I procured dinner that evening was peculiar. I was lying on the lawn on the flat of my back, when one of the Legation officials came up and asked me if I was ill. I replied that I was all right, except that I was frightfully hungry. He went off, and later on he and his wife made their appearance, very kindly bringing me something to eat and drink.

# CHAPTER V.

## THE LEGATIONS RELIEVED

During the night of August 14$^{th}$ the Legation Guards were relieved by the 7$^{th}$ Rajputs and others of the relieving force. They then made a hole through the wall of the Imperial Carriage Park, which formed the west boundary of the British Legation, and occupied it. It was the custom of the enemy to occupy the park during the day and harass the Legations by musketry fire, withdrawing regularly each night. The 23$^{rd}$ Royal Welsh Fusiliers were sent to hold it, and at dawn, when the Chinese came in to their barricades ignorant of our fresh position, they were allowed to come up to them, and were shot from the reverse side by the men awaiting them there.

Later in the morning we were sent to the Carriage Park to be quartered there, and posted our quarter guard at the main entrance facing north. Whilst standing there the sentry pointed out several Chinamen carrying arms, who were coming out from the houses on the north side of the British Legation. The guard turned out, as well as the officers present, and opened fire on them, and four were dropped in their tracks, the distance being 200 to 250 yards.

Heavy firing went on all the morning of the 15$^{th}$ to the west, as the Americans attacked the south gate of the Winter Palace, which they finally took. Captain Riley, 5$^{th}$ U.S. Artillery, was killed during the attack.

As the day wore on the firing gradually slackened, and the residents of the Legation, who had been confined for so long, came out into the park. They examined the State carriages in our quarters with interest, and some said that the last time they were used was at the marriage of the young Emperor. Curious antediluvian looking affairs they were, probably after a pattern designed by Confucius. The dragon-embroidered yellow satin hangings in them were very handsome. There was also the harness of some elephants lying about. It is said that at one time the Emperor possessed several of these animals, but as their arrival coincided with some national calamity, the wise men declared that as long as the animals remained the country would never prosper; so it was decided to put them to death. They were accordingly led outside the city, and there fastened up without food until they died.

There were several lofty buildings in the Carriage Park, and it was a matter of wonder to some of the besieged why the Chinese had never occupied the tops of their roofs, which commanded a considerable portion of the Legation. A Chinese mine was found in the park, which, if carried a few feet to the east, would have run under the western defences of the Legation, and when exploded must have caused great disaster. The story is that the Chinese ran their mine towards the wall, and hearing us countermining, became afraid, and ran their mine off in another direction. The mandarin in charge of the mine never went down it to inspect, but as he saw earth being regularly brought out, concluded it was all right.

We found a large number of embroidered silk cushions and mattresses in the Carriage Park, which came in very handy, as we had nothing with us except what we wore and carried on our chargers. The day was spent in various duties, escorts, guards, &c., and in getting the place into shape by removing barricades and so on. A large store of gunpowder was found in the rooms occupied by our quarter guard.

On the 16th we went out into the city, and found the foreign troops hard at work looting; men straggling about in every direction with boxes, furs, and ornaments. Parties were sent out under command of officers with orders to bring in what they could find to the Prize Committee, which was now started. One of these found a mandarin's house, and the store of wine and tinned provisions in it formed a welcome addition to the commissariat rations we had been living on for so long. Large quantities of furs and silks were also found, which went to the Prize Committee. Looting on the part of the British troops was carried on in the most orderly manner, and the houses of all those known to be friendly were protected.

It should be remembered that it is one of the unwritten laws of war that a city which does not surrender at the last and is taken by storm is looted. Numberless instances could be quoted, and considering the cowardly and unprovoked attack on the Legations, and the murder of Europeans, including helpless women and children, under circumstances of the most revolting cruelty, the Chinese were treated by us far better than they deserved. Many reports were current that the troops of other Powers, one in particular, shot every person they saw, armed or unarmed, whether man, woman, or child; but no instance of this ever came under my observation, beyond the fact that corpses of unarmed peasantry were seen lying about. The city was divided off into quarters, each of which was assigned to a European Power to police and look after.

On the 16<sup>th</sup> a detachment of my regiment, under Captain Parr, started with some guns, the Marines, and a body of French soldiers, to relieve the Peitang Cathedral, which had been holding out in the western portion of the city for several weeks, and from which no news had been received for many days, all communication between it and the Legations having been cut off. The place was taken during the day after some street fighting, in which our detachment had only one man wounded.

The garrison of the cathedral consisted of a few French and Italian marines, and the place contained nuns, priests, and numerous converts. The Chinese exploded two mines under the walls of the defences; one destroyed about eighty people, and the other one was nearly as disastrous. The defenders were running short of food when relieved. The place was held with the greatest gallantry by this small body of troops, assisted by Chinese Christians armed with sharpened sticks.

This expedition practically cleared the western portion of the city of Chinese troops and Boxers.

It was stated at first that the Empress left Pekin two days before we entered, but later intelligence states that she did not leave the palace until the 15$^{th}$, the day after our arrival. The Empress and Court, in common with other Chinese, believed that it was impossible we could ever enter Pekin, and I hear it was only when she saw the shells of the allies bursting in the courtyards, and her Chinese guards being struck down by bullets, that she realised that the game was up, and that it was time to bolt, which she is said to have done through the western gate of the palace, with only one attendant, travelling in a Pekin cart, and disguised as an ordinary individual, her journey for the first day or two being northwards. On entering the hills they turned south and made for Shansi. It was not until she had been travelling for several days that she reached her attendants, or had any personal comfort.

I believe the Chinese idea was that on the allied forces arriving before the city, they would demand its surrender, and halt while awaiting a reply. Instead of this, we forced our way in. The Chinese say that the people who looted Pekin were the Boxers, and that the European troops got but a small share. This is quite true. When the Boxer disturbances broke out, many people either removed or buried their valuables; the Boxers had the pick of what remained, and the allied forces got their leavings, except, of course, in the case of the houses of rich Boxers, temples, and Government buildings, which were found practically intact. The following incident is, in its way, instructive:-

The 24th Punjab Infantry were quartered in the Tartar city in the house of a wealthy Chinaman of rank. They had heard rumours that there was treasure buried in the vicinity, and searched, but did not find it. Six months later, when things had become more settled, the owner, with his wives, visited the house, and produced an order from the British headquarters authorising him to remove his property. On this he was allowed access. Proceeding to the room where the mess havildar* lived, he began to dig up the "koung," a raised platform at one end of the room, on which the havildar slept, and from under the tiles extracted numbers of silver shoes, blocks of silver worth about £4 each. The wives went off and dug in other rooms, and brought out small boxes, any amount of silver, and amongst other things a heavy iron safe. One wife dug and dug, but it was of no avail, nothing was there. After digging frantically for some time, she threw down her spade and sobbed heavily. Some one had anticipated her, and taken away what she had hidden. After this unaccustomed labour the ladies were rather fatigued, so the party repaired to the officers' mess and partook of some refreshment, and finally departed with their findings.

Later on, in the same vicinity, the colonel of the regiment issued orders that a certain well was to be cleaned out, and some Indian followers were told off to do it. Beneath the surface-rubbish at the bottom of the well a quantity of silver was found.

On August 18th a force, consisting of the 1st Bengal Lancers, one and one-half companies of the 7th Rajputs under

---

* Indian rank equivalent to sergeant.

Lieutenant Cutler, about two companies of the 24$^{th}$ Punjab Infantry, and two guns 12$^{th}$ Field Battery Royal Artillery, with whom were a detachment of the Hong Kong Maxim Battery, the whole under command of Lieutenant-Colonel Gartside Tipping, 1$^{st}$ Bengal Lancers, left the south gate of the Chinese city at 5 A.M. The force marched south towards the hunting park, and after entering and advancing about five hundred yards, halted. Half a company of the 7$^{th}$ Rajputs was left at the gate as a guard. The cavalry were sent out to the front and flanks to scout, and a party of them were charged by about a dozen Boxers who appeared from behind a fold of the ground. The cavalry killed about half of these, and the remainder fled, and joined a large body of the enemy, who appeared some eight hundred yards to their rear. The cavalry then cleared away from the front, the guns came into action, and one half company of the 7$^{th}$ Rajputs fired volleys at them. The enemy, after being fired at for some time, retired and disappeared towards the south. The cavalry then advanced to reconnoitre, and burnt a village which had been occupied by the enemy, but did not come into contact with them. They were reported to be about a thousand strong, and to have had some twenty casualties. The force then returned to Pekin.

The hunting park is a large open space of ground uncultivated, and surrounded by a wall with gateways, about ten miles in length from north to south, and from six to eight miles in breadth. It is known as the Imperial Hunting Park, being a game preserve of the Emperor's, distant about three miles from the south gate of the Chinese city. The Chinese kept a large number of troops in encampments there. Watered by one or more streams, it contains a number of villages. There are deer in the park, said to be of a rare species; they are spotted like the Indian Cheetul, or spotted deer, and have horns like a Ghooral's, an Indian wild goat, only rather longer and more massive, and are about the size of a fallow deer. There are some temples in the park.

A Japanese officer and a soldier, who were out in these grounds sometime after the reconnaissance just described, were murdered there, upon which the Japanese troops came down and destroyed twenty-one villages, the charred ruins of which are still standing. The Chinese understand drastic measures of this sort, and the result is that now were any stray Japanese to be belated by night in villages anywhere in the neighbourhood of Pekin, the villagers would probably help to defend them against any stray Chinese armed band that might come across them. The following incidents, though but indirectly connected with the relief of Pekin, are too interesting to be omitted.

On 15$^{th}$ August, during a cavalry reconnaissance near Tientsin, while retiring before a large body of Boxers, the horse of one of the American troopers suddenly came down, throwing its rider heavily. The Chinese soldiers dashed forward to secure him, when Lieutenant Gaussen, 1$^{st}$ Bengal Lancers, seeing how matters stood, at once rode back in the face of a heavy fire, took the American trooper on his horse, and brought him back into safety.

A German column under Major Von Hoepfner marched out on the 11$^{th}$ September to attack Liang-Hsian, about ten miles south of Liukachao, a half squadron 1$^{st}$ Bengal Lancers, and two Maxim guns; Hong-Kong and Singapore artillery co-operated. While the German infantry attack was developing, and while the city was under a heavy artillery fire, Captain Griffin moved forward on a flank, and came upon the Boxers streaming out of the city. He and his Lancers charged the enemy several times, his horse being shot under him; and while extricating himself from this position he was attacked by five Boxers. Trumpeter Sher Ali Khan of the 1$^{st}$ Bengal Lancers stood by him and shot four of them, thus saving the captain's life. The trumpeter was awarded the second class of the Order of Merit for this brave act.

News came early in September that an American force had been cut up between Tientsin and Pekin. Captain Browne, hearing of this, collected some twenty sowars, $1^{st}$ and $16^{th}$ B.L., and set off in aid. Before long the advanced scouts came in sight of two or three hundred armed men, shouting and waving swords and spears. Order was given to charge, and the enemy darted back into their village, which they had barricaded against mounted men. Captain Browne, however, effected an entrance on the farther side, and the enemy were cleared out and cut to pieces.

The American patrol were found to have taken refuge in some high crops, having lost one man.

# CHAPTER VI.

## THE FORBIDDEN CITY

On 28th August, a triumphal march of the allied forces through the Imperial Palace, known as the Forbidden City, took place.[1] There was much controversy as to what Power should take precedence of the others, and it was finally decided, so as to put an end to further disputes, that the troops should take precedence according to the strength of their respective armies in Pekin.

Rumour asserts that on this being settled at the council of generals, the Russian general turned to the Japanese commander and said, "How many troops have you?" "Eleven thousand," replied the Japanese, who, unfortunately for himself, had imbibed Western truthfulness with its civilisation. "I have fourteen thousand," replied the Russian, "and that settles it." Whether this be true or not, the Russians led the advance, and the Japanese with a more numerous force came second, the British third, followed by the Americans. A few days later it is said a council was held, at which military operations were discussed. "How many men have you?" asked a distinguished general of the Russian commander. "Five thousand men," was the reply. "I am profoundly astonished to hear it," was the rejoinder. "And why are you astonished?" asked the Russian. "I am astonished," he replied, "to hear that you have sent away as many as 9000 troops from Pekin within the last few days without our hearing anything about it." The Russian general was silent, and looked, or strove to look, as if nothing unusual had happened.

[1]The salute on this occasion was fired by the 12th Field Battery Royal Artillery with Chinese gunpowder recently unearthed.

*The front gate to the Forbidden City*

The palace is situated about the centre of Pekin, and is surrounded by high walls. By international agreement it was settled that no troops were to enter. The troops, therefore, seized and occupied the gates giving access to the palace and the guard-rooms above them. In the interior buildings were a number of Mandarin court officials, eunuch attendants, and probably some of the body-guard. It was given out before we went through that the Chinese officials inside would commit suicide on the hated foreigner entering the sacred precincts. However, instead of this gory spectacle meeting us on our entry, we found Mandarins and attendants clad in their best clothes, politely pointing out the way for us. True, they had a dejected, doleful aspect, but this may be accounted for by the fact of the officers having their swords drawn, and the men bayonets fixed, and their feeling doubts as to how the "foreign barbarian" would conduct himself on the occasion. Very different, indeed, were they to the lively, laughing attendants who, a few months later, conducted parties of officers and ladies round the buildings, occasionally making jokes.

The interior of the Winter Palace was interesting. Entering at the south gate, one passed through two extensive courtyards, separated by massive walls, which were connected by arched gateways. Over the gates which divided the two courts was a large building filled with racks, on which were thousands of bundles of arrows, ready feathered, and done up in tens, thousands of swords packed away in boxes, quivers, and other accoutrements for the archer, and numbers of bows. These formed, I hear, the equipment of the Imperial Palace Guard, who were not permitted to employ such modern innovations as the breech-loading rifle or the machine-gun.

At the farther end of the second court was a gateway guarded by an American sentry. Passing him, one entered the royal building, a series of squares, to which access was had by passing up a flight of stairs, going through a throne-room, and descending again on the farther side into another square. This was repeated two or three times, until one gained the palace garden, with the imperial joss-house* situated therein; and passing through the garden, left the palace by the north entrance. In the rooms thus passed through were beautiful large carpets worked with the imperial dragon. The throne, which in each room stood on a dais, was a large chair or couch capable of accommodating two. It was carved with dragons, and behind it was a screen, also carved with dragons. The ceiling had dragons painted and carved upon it; in fact, wherever you looked there were dragons carved, painted, or embroidered. A distinguished general once remarked, "I wonder the Chinese aren't all mad, what with making dragons and incessantly looking at them." The state rooms had been allowed to fall into disrepair. The beautiful carpets were covered in places with the dung of pigeons, numbers of which had taken up their abode in the buildings. Everything, too, was covered with a thick layer of dust, and the only things of any intrinsic value appeared to be some old cloisonné-work** urns and curious-shaped animals

* A temple with figures of deities.
** Layers of thin metal, to which enamels of various colours have been applied, set on a foundation plaque.

105

resembling the Burmese bilu or dragon.

The palace garden was carefully looked after. It was a picturesque and shady spot, and when we marched through on August 27$^{th}$ it appeared to be the coolest spot in Pekin. It contains the usual artificial rocks and grottoes that the Chinese delight in. The imperial joss-house was in perfect condition. The josses were well clothed in finely-embroidered robes, and in front of each were numerous dishes full of dried fruits, nuts, and bread. The rotundity of their paunches was remarkable, the paunch being reckoned among the Chinese as the seat of wisdom.

We were conducted round the palace by the Chinese officials left there when the Empress fled. After leaving the joss-house, we visited the private apartments of the Emperor and Empress, which are on the west side of the palace. The rooms were in good repair, but decorated in an extraordinary manner. One room had for ornaments a number of clocks in it, cuckoo-clocks, clocks with figures striking the hour, and other kinds. Another contained musical-boxes, mixed up with jade ornaments, thin slabs of jade carved with figures and fixed up in the windows so as to let the light shine through them. The carving of the woodwork screens and other fittings was beautiful, but taken altogether the exhibition was a disappointing one. One had expected something so very much better.

We saw the Emperor's and Empress's private sleeping apartments, which were in much the same style, the Emperor's rooms containing a small organ. There were a few Chinese maps about, and glass cases containing miniature trees, beneath which amber hares and deer disported themselves. A number of the imperial concubines were left in the palace; so the American officer of the palace guard told me. Hearing of this, two ladies who were one day going round the palace said they should like to call on them. The eunuchs vehemently protested that there were none; that they had all gone away; which, however, I am pretty sure was not the case, for it was reported shortly after that when the Chinese plenipotentiaries wanted the Emperor's seal to affix to some papers, they found that the Emperor had left it with one of the concubines, and so the Japanese who held the north gate were asked to get it from her, which they did.

Numbers of Chinese, both men and women, committed suicide on the entry of the Allies into the city, and officers have told me that they had seen whole families hanging by the neck. Suicide on such an occasion is, I believe, considered by the Chinese a meritorious act, and a sign of patriotism; in fact, much more worthy than going out and taking up arms to repel the invader, and falling on the field of battle in defence of one's country.

The Chinese are a curious people and difficult to understand. Our interpreter, Mr. Harris, who had long resided in the country, told us that formerly if a European went down the street, he was expected to get out of people's way, was jeered at, abused, and sometimes spat at. And now the people who did all this were civil, servilely civil. It was curious to see how well the Sepoys of the Indian army, Rajputs, Sikhs, and Punjabs, got on with them. These Sepoys policed the British quarter in the Chinese city, and did their duty well, as the orderly state of that portion of the city attested; it was under the control of a police commissioner, a captain of Bengal cavalry. The police appeared to be immensely popular, judging by the number of Chinese children one saw standing round them talking, laughing, and playing; a decided contrast to the police of other nationalities that are not far off. The American quarter adjoined ours, and was one of the best organised and policed of the whole lot.

*Street scene in Peking in 1860*

# CHAPTER VII.

## THE TEMPLE OF HEAVEN

It is doubtful if Pekin has ever been so clean since it was first founded. When we came here all the streets, except the largest main ones, were used as latrines, and the filth and smell to European eyes and noses was simply appalling; but soon the whole place was swept and kept clean, the roads mended, and places told off as latrines.

The railway, which under the old regime was not allowed to approach nearer to the walls of the city than three miles, now runs through the city walls, and the present terminus is right under the walls of that spot sacred to Chinese, the Temple of Heaven. I hear it is to be carried right on through the Chinese city into the Tartar city, and end in the vicinity of the Legations. So the halls and arches of the Winter Palace will re-echo to the shrill whistles of locomotives. The main streets have been lighted by oil-lamps hung on posts fixed to receive them.

The Temple of Heaven consists of an enclosure about a mile in length from east to west, and rather less from north to south. It is surrounded by a high wall, and access is obtained only on the western face by two gateways, about four hundred yards apart, each gateway having three arches in it closed by double doors. The main roads in it, which run to the principal buildings, are paved, and shaded by fine avenues of trees; large clusters and plantations of trees, many of which are very fine old cedars, cover a considerable part of the ground. It is said to be one of the most sacred places belonging to the Chinese, and has an inner and an outer enclosure. The outer enclosure contains the houses of the attendants and Mandarin in charge, and a bell tower containing a bell weighing several tons. The bell tower formed our mess. There is a joss-house in the outer enclosure, used as a Sepoys' cook-house, and the Hall of Harmony, where the burlesque which excited so much interest was performed, adjoins it. The inner enclosure contains a moated building, which became the quarters of the 16$^{th}$ Bengal Lancers, formerly the place where the Emperor stayed during his visits.

The following account, derived from Chinese visitors, is the best that I could get regarding the use to which the temple was put.

The Emperor, who is also high priest, used to visit the Temple of Heaven once every six months. On the day of his progress the Chien-men road, which runs from the Winter Palace to the temple, was sprinkled with yellow sand, and the cross streets running into it were walled up so that no one might interfere with the royal procession.

On arrival at the temple he was accommodated in the building occupied by the 16$^{th}$ Bengal Lancers. He stayed there for the night, and during the day visited the Hall of Harmony, where musicians played to him - judging by the instruments found there, chiefly on bells, drums, and gigantic violins.

At night he visited the sacred buildings, and repaired to the Temple of the Sun, where he prostrated himself thirty-seven times, striking his head each time on the pavement. Then proceeding to the Temple of the Moon, he awaited there the auspicious moment. On this being announced, by the priests I presume, he went to the Temple of Heaven, also called by some the centre of the Universe, and there, on the summit of the circular marble terraces, communed with the God of Heaven. Ten newly decapitated heads of oxen were placed around him in a circle, and were offered at some period of the service on the sacrificial altar close by. Three lanterns were lit and hoisted on the three lofty masts, to announce to the outside world what was taking place. This service occurred at night. Articles of some different nature were sacrificed in the urns, constructed of open iron work just below the platform. The ceremonies now were completed, and the Emperor returned to the palace.

Of recent years, with but one or two exceptions, no European has been permitted inside the gates of the outer enclosure. The place was closed also to the majority of the Chinese.

The Temple of the Sun is a circular, wooden structure, standing on the top of several handsome marble terraces, also circular. It is connected by an elevated and broad terrace with the Temple of the Moon. This terrace is, some think, the best part of the T. of H., as we called it. It looks magnificent, and even the grass-farm haystacks with which it is cumbered at present cannot altogether destroy its appearance.

The Temple of the Moon is a smaller and less imposing structure than that of the Sun. The entrance to it is situated on the side farthest away from the Temple of the Sun, and faces a series of circular marble terraces rising one above the other - the Temple of Heaven. A curious feature in this temple is the absence for the most part of the stone screen which invariably fronts a Chinaman's door, and is either inside or outside the yard, and may be of wood or stone or other material. The object of this screen is, I am told, to exclude devils, the Chinaman being so simple-minded as to believe that a devil can only go straight, and that on his making for his house he is brought up by the screen, and so discouraged thereby that he gives up the attempt. This is but one of the many instances of the opposite views of ourselves and of the Chinese race, for to our ideas a devil is by no means simple-minded, nor are his ways straight.

The cook-house of the Rajputs in the Temple of Heaven was a curious sight. The cooks stooping over their small wood and coal fires, and the men sitting round eating, while towering above them through the gloom and smoke the figures of the Chinese gods were seen looking down. The cook-house used to be the joss-house. All the josses that were light enough to move had been carefully put away on one side, and only the big figures remained. The large figures are made of wood, and on examination were found to be hollow inside. The insides were stuffed with prayer rolls, while from their necks hung by a hook a silk bag, which, on being opened, was found to contain heart, lungs, liver, &c., made of lead and tinted the correct colour; a stomach made of silk-piping carefully coiled up and stuffed with grain of various sorts, and in some a small silk bag attached, with "this is the secret bag" written on it, which, when opened, was found to contain copper cash, beads, bits of amber, and a few seed pearls.

It was impossible for any one with military training to be in contact with so many foreign troops day after day without forming some opinion of them, and it is remarkable how unanimous were the conclusions arrived at. Even Jack Sepoy had his ideas as to the merits of the foreigners.

He said he could get on well with all the troops except the Frenchmen. He found the Americans, Japanese, Russians and Italians friendly; they talked together by signs when on guard or duty near each other, and showed one another their equipment and rifles; but the Frenchman, if asked to see his rifle, or made any other advances towards him, was suspicious and surly.

The French troops with which our men were most in contact were those present during the advance, and consisted of regiments from Tonquin, marines, I believe. They were inferior to the troops which they have now in the country, both as regards discipline and appearance. The Zouaves,* Chasseurs d'Afrique* and others compare favourably with any other troops. The Russian is a tough, hardy man, without much "bundobust" (arrangement) for the care of the men. The Japanese are very brave, and just like Ghurkas, with a wonderful "bundobust." The Italian is a good soldier. The German is a prodigy at drill. As to the American, I can't get any definite opinion. The Sepoy critic knows that they are our friends, and says "Sahib Logue Ki Muafik," which means "like an Englishman of a good class." The German troops here drill splendidly in close order formations; their sentries are smart at saluting, and at their duties generally.

From what we saw of their troops at manoeuvres, their generals appear to move considerable bodies of troops with great precision, each regiment being in its right place and coming up at the right time. Though some of their formations in the attack appear, by the light thrown on the subject by the Boer war, to be open to criticism, there are certain details in their field work which we might follow with advantage. Amongst others, every man when on the defensive has a rest for his rifle, a few stones or sods of earth placed in front, which to a certain extent conceal him from view. Their attack is carried home right into their enemy's position, and their gunners only stand up when actually serving the gun; at all other times they crouch down on the ground.

On the other hand, the second line advancing in close order to reinforce the firing line during the attack, and performing the high step previous to reaching it, seems to be utterly out of place; the more so as immediately before

* Zouaves were raised in Algeria, but later recruited from other parts of the French Empire. Chasseurs d'Afrique were first raised in metropolitan France for service in North Africa.

115

reaching the firing line, they break up into open order and disperse among it.

There appears to be no standing or kneeling, as with us, during the attack; at every halt the men lie down; they move at a quick, a very quick walk, with rifles at the short trail when at some distance from the point attacked; as they get nearer they advance by rushes, no steady double, but a quick rush as fast as they can go. Their men are not as well dressed as ours, their uniforms fit badly, and this remark applies equally to all the other foreign troops. It is a question, however, whether our uniforms generally, but especially as regards the seat of "Tommy's" trousers, are not cut too tight to be thoroughly serviceable.

The physique of the Germans was about the average of the Allies. The Russians appeared to be a fine set of men, broad shouldered, sturdily built, and full of endurance; rough and ready, but ignorant, lacking in intelligence, and brutal in the hour of victory.

The French can be divided into two classes: their good troops and their bad. In the first come the Chasseurs d'Afrique, Zouaves, and a few other regiments. In the second their Marines, and corps recruited from the slums of Paris. The discipline of the former appeared to be good, and the men a fine, soldierly looking lot. The discipline of the latter was, one has no hesitation in saying so, the worst in the allied army. Slovenly, disgracefully dressed, insolent when opportunity offered, and insubordinate, they appeared to be totally lacking in all soldierly instincts. Even their friends the Russians, when asked what they thought of them, simply shrugged their shoulders.

The Japanese troops appear to be well disciplined, and their men are very hardy and enduring. I believe that the

Russians who were out here have changed their opinion regarding them considerably, and by no means look forward to a conflict with them with the keenness they once felt.

The Japanese are undoubtedly superior to the Russians in education and intelligence, while as regards individual courage, organisation, equipment, and training they are in no way inferior.

One saw but little of the Italian troops, but those that were seen gave the impression of being of good physique, well turned out, and soldierly.

The Americans have a different standard of discipline to that of our men; they appear to be much more free and easy in their relation to their officers, and in the way they performed their duties; still they have a discipline, and that of a rigid kind, otherwise the sight of a soldier walking down a street of Pekin, with his hands held high, followed by an American officer with a revolver pointed at the back of his head, both moving towards a guard, could not have occurred. The American soldier appears to be very intelligent, independent, and able to act on his own initiative.

The Indian troops compared favourably as regards discipline with the Allies. In marching power under a hot sun they naturally excelled; they did not get out of hand after the capture of Pekin, nor did they commit atrocities, while, as regards soldierly bearing and turn out, they stood first. Thus the numerous guards, sentries, and orderlies of the 1$^{st}$ Sikhs at the Summer Palace were far smarter, better dressed, and superior in appearance to any guards or orderlies that the Allied Powers could produce in Pekin, not excepting the guards at their Legations, which, it is presumed, were of picked men. So, too, the guard of the Royal Welsh Fusiliers at the British Legation was far superior to that of any other nationality.

# CHAPTER VIII.

## COLOURS IN THE FIELD

The British practice of carrying no colours in the field appeared at one time to be likely to cause serious inconvenience. We started without any colours, but by the time we arrived at Pekin the Lieutenant-General had a Union Jack carried with him, every squadron of cavalry carried one, and most of the infantry regiments carried one or two rolled up and ready for use. They were absolutely necessary, both for display to prevent any of our allies firing on us, as it is extremely difficult to ascertain to what men belong who are in khaki, even when at no great distance, and also for hoisting on any gate or other place captured by British troops. If this was not done, the troops of the nationality next arriving promptly hoisted theirs. All the foreign troops had colours with them.

It seems probable that before long colours, or, at any rate, the national ensign, will have to be carried by us in the field. All foreigners appear to be adopting khaki; the British, Americans, Japanese, Germans, Austrians, and French were all wearing it at Pekin within eight months of their arrival there; and when the day comes that opposing armies in the field are both khaki clad, it will result in a choice of evils, whether colours shall be carried, with the result of more or less drawing the enemy's fire, or whether they shall not be carried, in which case it is pretty certain that our men will often be fired on by our own side.

Sepoys who wore the Kilmarnock cap* complained that it

---

* A cap fitting closely around the brows but large and full above. Otherwise known as a Scotch bonnet or a Tam-O'-Shanter (as in the poem by Robert Burns).

was little protection from the sun in summer, while in winter it afforded them no warmth at all.

The enormous pugarees worn by the Sepoys of many regiments of the Indian army, though presenting an imposing appearance on parade, prove a useless encumbrance in the field; they nullify to a great extent the advantage of cover, and are unnecessarily heavy and burdensome on the march. A very much smaller pugaree would suffice for protection against the sun in summer or the cold in winter, and would render the wearer more comfortable and less conspicuous.

The Chinese are such bad shots that no deductions could be drawn as to the relative merits of solah topees and pugarees as a headgear in action for British officers with native troops. It was pretty clear that an officer who could wear a pugaree throughout the advance on Pekin must have been exceptionally sun proof; there may possibly have been one or two who did so, but it is doubtful. A very large proportion of officers wore solah topees, and even then felt the intense heat they were exposed to.

The shooting of the Indian army would be much improved were all the men to wear a sun-shade made in the shape of a leather hat peak, and tied on to the head with a string, so as to shelter the eyes when firing and on outpost and other duties where a clear view is necessary. This shade should be part of the equipment of every soldier. It is used almost universally by Persians when shooting or travelling, and when not in use is slung round the neck like a gorget,* or carried slung by its string over one shoulder, and hanging under the opposite arm. It is shaped like a quarter moon, with an eyelet hole at each of the two horns of the crescent, to which the fastening string or leather lace is attached. Any one who has fired at a

---

* A piece of armour to protect the throat, or a neck ornament.

target or at game in a pugaree, or with his hat off, when the sun is facing him in the direction in which he fires, will agree with the necessity that exists for some kind of eye shade.

The German troops in Pekin came there with two kinds of headgear; one a solah topee, and the other a C.I.V. hat* made of straw. This latter was found to afford insufficient protection, and later on both the above patterns of headgear were withdrawn and a helmet was substituted, which came further down on the head than our Indian pattern does, and afforded more protection to the temples and face; the back part of it juts out straighter than in ours, and affords little or no obstacle to a man firing in it in the lying down position, an impossibility in ours. The back part has two or three longitudinal divisions in it, and the whole of this can be turned up towards the top of the helmet. I have frequently seen it worn in this position, when it does not overbalance and fall off the wearer's head, as I have heard stated. In this one instance the Germans seem to have hit off something in tropical equipment which is decidedly better than anything of ours.

The officers' sword hilts of the present fashion were most conspicuous, flashing almost like heliographs** at times. The buttons and brass shoulder badges on the khaki uniform all tend to frustrate one of its objects, *i.e.* invisibility, while the magazine of the Lee-Metford was found on occasions to tear off the shoulder badges.

The followers of the Indian army had exactly the same pattern of winter clothing issued them as the Sepoys. Any one

---

* The City Imperial Volunteers (CIV) was the name given to the regiment which had been raised by the City of London at the beginning of 1900 to form part of the forces fighting the Boers in South Africa. The regiment's wide brimmed hats were similar to those in summer use in the Germany Army.

** Apparatus for signalling by means of a moveable mirror reflecting flashes of sunlight to a distance.

acquainted with India is aware how utterly filthy and disreputable the Indian coolie becomes, as was especially the case with us when, on account of the cold, he wore his clothing day and night for months, and did coal and other fatigues in them. Many foreigners used to mistake, or possibly pretended to mistake, the followers for Sepoys, and thus got the idea that they were an untidy and unsoldierly lot.

In order to avoid such mistakes in future, it might be well to clothe the followers in a different manner to the Sepoys, as regards colour or shape of garment; the more so, as united action by the European Powers against offenders of international law will probably be more frequent in the future, and the Indian army will be taking its share in them.

There is a tendency to do away with as many followers as possible in the Indian army when in the field. Care, however, should be taken that they are not reduced to such a point as to impair efficiency.

The number of cooks allowed in a native regiment is sixteen, or two per company. This is the minimum number that suffices, but it is pretty certain that during a campaign of any length there will be casualties amongst them, and apart from this there may be numerous detachments and guards sent out, when, even if the cooks are at their full number, they will be insufficient, with the result that men who are already hard worked will have to devote several hours a day to cooking their own food. As it happened, we started for China with a full complement, but owing to sickness and death we became short-handed, and during the winter in North China it was impossible to replace them, very great inconvenience was experienced accordingly.

Barbers, too, are necessary for cutting the men's hair, and, what is more important, their toe-nails. Natives are unable to do this themselves, and the neglect of it may seriously affect the men's marching powers, as ingrowing nails and other evils may ensue.

No *dhobies* (washermen) are allowed now on service, but the regulations do not say how the men are to keep their clothes clean during a stay of a year or so in a foreign country. Fortunately there are ways and means by which even this regulation can be evaded; were it not so, we might have deserved the taunts some of the French newspaper writers, and French officers too, who should have known better, threw at us.

Stories have appeared in the papers, I am told, written by newspaper correspondents, saying how barbarously the Chinese were treated by our troops, that men, women, and children were slain by them. I believe that as regards our soldiers, both British and native, such stories are absolutely devoid of truth. I never saw an instance, nor heard of one, in which our men killed either women or children. Of course in street fighting, where there are armed men mixed up with unarmed, and stray women or children happen to be about, they are always liable to be hit. A correspondent following the force, say a day or two later, and finding corpses of women and children lying about, as I hear they were, might erroneously attribute their slaughter to our men. I have been told of cases in which Japanese coolies, following in rear of the army, decapitated aged men and women whom the troops in their passage on had spared. It was stated on our landing at Taku that no Chinese coolies could be procured to assist in unloading stores, &c., as the Russians shot every Chinaman they saw.

Russian methods are summary, and those who have read the history of the taking of Geok Teppe* in their campaign

* The reference is to the sack of that fortress in 1881 by Russian troops under the command of General Skobelev. It is said that 8,000 defenders and civilians were killed while fleeing across the desert, and that a further 6,500 were killed within the fortress.

against the Turkomans will not be surprised at a good deal of unnecessary slaughter being attributed to them.

An officer of rank and experience once said to me, "You can divide the troops in China into two classes, the civilised and the uncivilised; the civilised are the English, Americans, and Japanese." Many of us here will agree with him.

The German troops were naturally exasperated at the murder of their minister, and the character of their send-off from Germany was hardly of a nature calculated to allay this feeling. The quarter of Pekin policed by them took longer to settle down than that of any other nationality. For weeks and weeks while the Japanese, American, and English quarters were peaceably settled, the shops open and numerous stalls in the street, the German quarter was practically deserted.

Strange indeed was the change that came over Pekin in the last few months of its occupation. Whereas the first time I went down the Chien-men Road on August 15$^{th}$, 1900, there were blazing houses, corpses lying about, and a few people who as soon as they caught sight of troops slid round the corners. Not many weeks later the road was crowded with Chinamen from end to end selling every kind of goods at stalls in the street, feeding at open-air restaurants, while peep-shows, bands, reciters, acrobats, and fortune-tellers were surrounded by crowded audiences. The children no longer, as in the old days, cried "foreign devil" on seeing a European, but called after the man wearing British or American uniform "Number one, number one," the Chinese expression for excellence, and "Houdi, houdi", "Good, good." Perhaps they had begun to find out that the foreign devil is not such a bad devil after all.

# CHAPTER IX.

## BROKEN BITS OF CHINA

### I.

One of the stories current in Pekin was to the effect that in the early days of the Boxer movement the Empress sent a prince to their leaders to test the correctness or otherwise of the statement that they and their followers were invulnerable to bullets. The leaders having heard what was to happen took measures accordingly. Previous to the arrival of the prince they had one party prepared with loaded rifles to fire at another. The men who were to fire had extracted the bullets from their cartridges, which bullets were given to the men to be fired at to hold in their mouths. One the prince's arrival and on their being fired at with the blank cartridges they spat the bullets out. The prince witnessing this was quite satisfied as to their bullet-proof qualities, and returning to the Empress reported accordingly.

A council was held in the palace later on at which numerous dignitaries were present, and it was decided to go to war with all the European Powers. The Emperor, it is said, expostulated with the Dowager Empress, saying, "We might go to war with one or two, or perhaps even three, of the foreign nations, but how can we fight against the whole lot?" The Empress became very angry and replied, "You forget that the Boxers are with us this time, that they are invulnerable, and that the more foreign nations come against us the better, as then we shall destroy the whole lot 'at one sitting'."

### II.

The tactics of the Chinese are peculiar; many of their

maxims on war date from the time of Confucius (Kung-fusis). Men who were present during the siege of Tientsin Foreign Settlement say that when the Chinese advanced to a night attack each man carried two lanterns. The Europeans that night on outpost duty saw an immense line of lanterns advancing towards the settlement. The troops turned out and awaited the illuminated line which was gradually approaching. When considered sufficiently near, fire was opened, and the lanterns were seen rising in the air and falling to the ground, in fact in any position except advancing. Needless to observe, the attack was easily repulsed. It was afterwards found that the Chinese had simply been acting according to one of their ancient precepts, which lays down that in a night attack each soldier should carry two lanterns, one in each hand, by which means the enemy would think that the attacking force is double its actual strength, and be so terrified at having to encounter such an altogether unanticipated and overwhelming force as to fly on their approach.

The Chinese art of war is apparently based on a theory that if you only terrify your enemy sufficiently you will gain an easy victory, without having to strike a single blow. The Chinese are fond of using crackers on the field of battle. These are strings of small paper cartridges, with one hundred or more in a string. When let off they sound exactly like rapid independent firing, and can be made either to imitate the loud and sustained roar of a hot infantry fire, or else to die fitfully away in a few isolated shots, and revive again as required. One's first impression on hearing them fired during an engagement is that there must be a hot fight going on where the sound comes from, and when the noise every now and then dies away into a few shots and again bursts out with renewed vigour, it seems that the troops firing must be well in hand.

Another Chinese maxim is that, when camping at night, as many fires should be lit as possible, to induce the enemy to

126

suppose them to be in far greater strength than is actually the case.

It is said that in the war with China during the sixties, the Chinese erected paper forts of immense size on the line of advance of the invading column, in the hopes of deterring them. Also that sailing junks had paddles and paddle-boxes put on them, the paddles being turned by men working the crank connecting them; that funnels were put on the junks and fires lit beneath them to give us the idea that they had steamboats in their fleet. It is also stated that the Chinese were much astonished at our entering Pekin at once, and pressing on into the city without any delay. The Chinese mind reasoned that, as in the sixties we had halted outside of Pekin and given them twenty-four hours in which to capitulate, we should do the same on this occasion, omitting to take into consideration the different circumstances of the two cases. This would account for the large number of inhabitants, men and women, that were seen running out of their houses as the troops advanced through the city, the people apparently being taken by surprise - doors of shops being left open, and fires with kettles boiling or meals cooking being seen in the houses.

It is said, I do not know with what truth, that the generals and chief officers were always the first to quit the field of battle, and that on some occasions the general used to quit the day before the fight.

### III.

When stationed in the Temple of Heaven the troops often paraded on the open space outside it, and there it was no uncommon sight to see the following all going on at the same time: the Indian infantry doing the attack; the German infantry practising the march past; the American Field Battery doing gun drill, while their cavalry exercised their horses in the vicinity; the French troops route marching down the road which ran

127

*The Summer Palace*

through the middle of the ground; while the Japanese "Transportation" guard close by looked on!

## IV.

On the incoming of the Chinese winter - which by the way is very severe in the Chili province - there were several amusing incidents.

One morning the mess dhobie (washerman) came to me with one of the mess tablecloths rolled up into the shape of a long roll, and frozen solid. "Sahib," he said, "this is my petition. Yesterday I went down to the city ditch as usual to wash. I broke the ice and entered the water; it was frightfully cold. I washed the clothes as usual and wrung them out, and this - producing the cloth - is the result. What am I to do when clothes get all hard like this?"

On another occasion the bhistie (water-carrier) complained that the water in his mussuck (leather water-bag) had turned into a solid block of ice so that he could not pour any water out, and that the mussuck was so cold that it made him ill to carry it.

These complaints were remedied as soon as the houses for heating water and washing were ready, while the dhobie was provided with a small hand-cart, though even this did not prevent the water from getting frozen if it was left standing any length of time. These men, and a great number of the sepoys, came from the north-west provinces of India, where it seldom reaches freezing-point and where snow is unknown. Consequently they had never seen solid masses of ice beyond the artificially-made pieces used for cooling purposes in hot weather.

An officer's orderly once hurried into his room and said: "Sahib, there is the most extraordinary 'tamasha' (spectacle) going on outside." "What is it?" inquired the officer. "It is the most wonderful thing I have ever seen. I can't describe it; come and see." The officer left his room - which, by the way, had paper windows - and went outside. "This," said the orderly, with a wave of his hand including the sky and the ground, "is the wonderful thing." It was snowing.

The sepoys, as is customary in their own country, were fond of dropping water about and emptying "lotahs" (brass pots) on the steps outside their quarters, and on the ramps leading down from their guard-rooms on the city walls. This rapidly converted them into dangerous slides, and it was not until after some unpleasant experiences, and the issue of orders against such practices, that it stopped.

The climate of China, in the Chili province, compares favourably with that of India. The really hot season is July, August, and September; the heat at midday can be borne without a punkah, though the thermometer rises to 105° in the shade. October and November are pleasant. December, January, and February are cold. In January the thermometer falls below zero. The end of March, April, and May are pleasant; June is hot. The nights are always cool. The curses of the country are the house flies in summer, and the winds that blow spring, autumn, and winter, carrying clouds of dust with them. In winter these winds chill one to the bone, and hands or ears left uncovered are liable to be frost-bitten. The rainy season is June, July, and August, but long continued breaks are plentiful. The winter, when - I say when advisedly - the wind is not blowing, is very pleasant. A fine, warm sun shines overhead for a few hours in the middle of the day, while it freezes hard in the shade. The climate in the summer on the sea-coast is quite pleasant, owing to sea breezes off the cold water of the Gulf of Chili. Judging by the robust appearance of the inhabitants, the climate must be a healthy one to live in, with but three months of hot weather instead of six as in India.

# V.

The Americans, who were quartered in the Temple of Agriculture, about 400 yards from the Temple of Heaven, had one curious custom. All their dead lying in out-of-the-way villages or other places were brought in and buried close to their posts, which were held by troops. When the campaign was over the coffins were exhumed and shipped to the United States. As one American officer put it: "Every American mother who sends a son on a campaign receives him back either alive or in a casket."

Soon after our arrival in Pekin General Chaffee, commanding the United States troops, held a review. This took place on the open ground between the Temples of Heaven and Agriculture. It was an interesting sight, and an immense number of officers of all nationalities assembled as spectators, forming a dense line just in rear of the saluting point. The march past was very effective. Each regiment of infantry marched past headed by its colours and its band. All the men were in the uniforms they had worn during the campaign, and they looked most workman-like. Of the regiments on the ground at least one had never been in cantonments, but had been fighting ever since it was raised for service in Cuba, whence it was sent to the Philippines,* thence on to China, and when I last saw it it was under orders to return to the Philippines.

The bands played well, and the men tramped past with a steady swing, the brilliant colours of the silken stars and stripes that waved above them forming a striking contrast to the dull coloured lines of slouch-hatted, blue-jerseyed, khaki-trousered men that followed them.

---

* The Spanish-American War (1898) had resulted in the expulsion of Spain from Cuba and the Philippines, but United States forces were subsequently engaged against Philippine nationalists.

In one regiment the officers carried no swords. I learnt afterwards that they had found them useless in the Philippines, and had left them there.

The cavalry and guns followed the infantry, but one saw little of them owing to the immense clouds of dust they raised. The review was decidedly a success, and impressed those who saw it.

A review held in a country in peace time, and one held in the enemy's capital by troops who have captured it after a short though trying campaign, are two very different things to the spectator. In the first case he criticises the dress and turn-out of the men, the accuracy of manoeuvre, and precision of drill and dressing. In the second, he knows what the troops before him have gone through, and understands that the polished button, pipe-clayed belt, and well-blacked boot - the absence of which in peace time would damn a regiment for ever - have all disappeared as completely as if they never had been, under the stern exigencies of war. He criticises now the physique, condition, and bearing of the men, and how they appear to have stood the test they have gone through; how they move as bodies of armed men.

## VI.

The Summer Palace stands about six miles north-west of Pekin, at the foot of and amongst some low hills, offshoots of the great range close by to the west.

It is one of the most beautiful places I have ever seen, and is built on the northern side of a large lake covering one or two square miles. In the lake was an island covered with buildings, reached by a bridge in profile like a highly-strung bow, the surface of the water representing the string. It starts on each side with low arches eight to ten feet high, and then with higher ones and higher, until the centre arch of the bridge must be from thirty to forty feet above the water. The distant hills were in places crowned by pagodas, evidently placed there for artistic effect; while the palace itself consisted of an immense number of separate buildings, some near the water's edge, and others studded over the low hill just beyond. The whole hill laid out as a garden, and its apex crowned by a temple to Buddha, looked magnificent.

The handsome yellow-tiled roofs of the Imperial quarters, surmounted by quaint-looking animals as part of the ridge tiles, glistened in the sun. Along the northern edge of the lake ran a handsome marble wall with a balustrade, and numerous steps leading down to the water's edge, and at intervals stood handsome open shelters - roofs erected on pillars over marble platforms. Bronze urns and dragons stood about the place in front of the more important buildings, on pedestals. Paths wound about and up and down the hillside to the various houses; occasionally they ran through grottos artificially constructed, and in one part of the garden was a regular labyrinth of paths running through what appeared at first sight to be natural caverns. Every atom of a small temple, including the furniture, was made of bronze. Many of the houses were greatly damaged, but not by our troops. On the lake floated numerous boats, steam launches, ships' boats, and a number of Chinese boats, the stems of which ended off like a small tree with boughs shooting out and leaves stuck on to them. Then there was a marble boat - in reality a two-storied apartment built on a marble platform, shaped to resemble a boat, and standing up out of the water. The palace had been, I was told, fitted with electric light, but the plant for this had been removed before my visit. Italian troops had been quartered in some of the buildings, but the British troops there (the 12th Field Battery and the 1st Sikhs) were in houses outside.

One building in the palace had a Sikh sentry over it, and

in this were stored a number of curios - bronzes, cloisonne, jade ornaments, &c. - which the British on occupying the palace had found scattered about. These were, later on, handed over to the Chinese Government. The officer in charge of these found a catalogue describing many of the things, and some of the bronzes were there shown as being more than two thousand years old.

The first troops, I understand, to arrive at the palace were the Japanese and the Russians; anyhow, one lot arrived soon after the other, and they were in occupation for some days before any of our troops were sent there. Cartloads of valuables were carried away - silks, cloisonne, bronzes, clocks, &c. On the farther slope of the palace ridge of hills, *i.e.* the slope away from the lake, stood the ruins of the old Summer Palace, looted and burned in the sixties as a punishment for the duplicity of the Chinese in treacherously seizing the peace envoys of the allied British and French armies, whom they tortured so cruelly that but few survived.

## VII.

Soon after our arrival in Pekin one of the senior native officers, Subadar Ram Ratan Singh, caught malarial fever, and died within three days. He was followed on the 24th of October by Subadar Major Gurdatt Singh Bahadur, who died of dysentery. The Subadar Major is, I should explain, the senior native officer of a regiment, and his title of "Bahadur" was conferred on him on the occasion of his visit to England at the close of the Egyptian Campaign of 1882, when her Majesty Queen Victoria personally decorated him with the Second Class of the Order of British India. He was exceptionally well educated, and was the only native officer in the Indian Army holding an "extra" musketry certificate. Both these officers were a great loss to the regiment, and their deaths were no doubt attributable to the trying nature of the advance on Pekin, from which neither - both being pretty well advanced in years - completely recovered. The Subadar Major died after being transferred to Wei-Hei-Wei; Subadar Ram Ratan Singh at Pekin. As a mark of respect to the latter, an old soldier who had served in the regiment ever since he enlisted, the British officers of the regiment adopted the unusual course of attending his funeral. This took place during a heavy shower of rain. The body wrapped in a white sheet was laid on a native bed, or charpoy, and was borne on the shoulders of sepoys to the burning place, as he was a Hindu. The British and native officers followed. On arriving at the city gate the British officers halted and saluted, while the remains of the fine old Subadar, surrounded by native officers and sepoys, passed on to the final scene, which took place on the banks of the city moat close by.

A native soldier's funeral takes place without any military ceremony, the soldiers attending being attired in their native dress. The striking part of the ceremony to a European is its extreme simplicity. Native Christian soldiers are buried with all the usual ceremony that attends that of a Britisher.

## VIII.

The Australian Naval Contingent landed after the occupation of Pekin. There were about five hundred of them, and half were stationed in Pekin. They were a fine sturdy lot of men, who wore the British Naval uniform - none very young, but all a well-seasoned lot - just the sort of men one likes to have by one in a row. There were a large number of old man-of-war's men amongst them. The marines who accompanied them were known as the "horse marines." These were part of a corps of bushrangers collected for service in South Africa, but more were collected than the Government required, and so they did not know what to do with them. However, on a naval contingent being offered for service in China and accepted, the bright idea struck the Australians of sending the surplus bushrangers with it as marines. So to China they went; but although termed "marines," they still retained the uniform they were equipped with for South Africa, and serviceable and soldierly they looked in their felt hats with looped-up brim, khaki-coloured suits, bandoliers, and riding-breeches.

# APPENDIX A
## Summary of Killed and Wounded during the Advance on and Relief of Peking.
### BRITISH FORCE

| CORPS | PEITSANG. | | YANGTSUN. | | Between 8th and 14th August | | Between 16th and 20th August | | TOTAL | |
|---|---|---|---|---|---|---|---|---|---|---|
| | Killed | Wounded | Killed | Wounded | Killed | Wounded | Killed | Wounded | Killed | Wounded |
| No. 12 F.B., Royal Artillery | – | 3 | – | – | 1 | – | – | – | | |
| Royal Marine Light Infantry | – | – | 2 | 8 | – | – | – | – | | |
| 2nd Batt. Royal Welsh Fusiliers | – | 1 | – | – | – | – | – | 2* | | |
| 1st Bengal Lancers | – | 3 | – | – | – | 2 | – | 1 | | |
| 7th Rajputs | 1 | 4 | 5 | 20* | – | 1 | – | – | | |
| 1st Sikhs | 1 | 5 | 1 | 10 | 1 | 2 | – | – | | |
| 24th Punjab Infantry | – | 2 | – | – | – | – | – | – | | |
| H.K.S. Batt., Royal Artillery | – | 2 | – | – | – | – | – | – | | |
| Hong Kong Regiment | – | 4 | – | – | – | – | – | – | | |
| Total | 2 | 24 | 8 | 38 | 2 | 5 | – | 3 | 12 | 70 |

* One British officer (1st Sikhs) dangerously, and one 1st Bengal Lancers slightly wounded.

The losses of our Allies, as far as can be ascertained, were as follows:-

Peitsang – Japanese, 300 killed and wounded; Americans unknown; Russians and French, 6 wounded.
Yangtsun – Japanese, none; Americans, about 40 to 50; Russians, 27 killed and wounded; French, none.
Capture of Peking – Russians, 26 killed, 102 wounded; Japanese, 200 killed and wounded; Americans and French, unknown.

# APPENDIX B

*Extract from a Despatch by Sir Claude Macdonald,
dated December 24<sup>th</sup>, 1900*

"At about 2 A.M. there was a pause, when very distinctly the delighted garrison heard the boom of heavier guns away to the east, and the sound of many Maxims evidently outside the City Walls. The scene in the Legation was indescribable. Those who, tired out, had fallen asleep were wakened by these unwonted sounds, and there was much cheering and shaking of hands. The enemy too had heard it . . . . Shortly before 3 P.M. a breathless messenger from the Tartar City Wall arrived to say that foreign troops were under the City Wall opposite the Water Gate. I immediately followed him, and arrived in time to receive General Gaselee and his staff as they came through the said gate and stood on the Canal Road. From there I led them through the Russian Legation to the British, where they were welcomed by the rest of the besieged garrison. The regiment which first entered the Legation Quarter was the 7$^{th}$ Rajputs under Major Vaughan. With them was Major Scott of the 3$^{rd}$ Sikhs, attached to the 1$^{st}$ Sikhs, with a few men of this regiment. This officer with several men ran along the Canal Road from the south bridge to the gateway opposite the First Secretary's house, and they were the first to enter the British Legation."

# SELECTIVE BIBLIOGRAPHY

This brief guide is intended to help the reader who may wish to follow up subjects raised in this book. It is not, of course, by any means comprehensive.

Peter Fleming, *The Siege at Peking*,
Oxford University Press, 1984.

Alan J. Guy and Peter B. Boyden,
*Soldiers of the Raj, The Indian Army 1600-1947.*
This book, published by the National Army Museum in association with its Special Exhibition on the subject which opened in August 1997, but much more than a simple catalogue, contains a "Guide to Further Reading" which provides an extensive list, with evaluations, of books and articles on the Indian Army.

Peter Hopkirk, *The Great Game*,
Oxford University Press, 1991.

Immanuel C.Y. Hsu, *The Rise of Modern China*,
Oxford University Press, 2000.

Lawrence James, *Raj*,
Little, Brown and Company, 1997.

Henry Keown-Boyd, *The Fists of Righteous Harmony*,
Leo Cooper, 1991.

Richard O'Connor, *The Boxer Rebellion*,
Hale, 1974

Diana Preston, *Besieged in Peking*,
Constable, 1999.

H.G. Rawlinson, *The History of the $3^{rd}$ Battalion $7^{th}$ Rajput Regiment – Duke of Connaught's Own*,
Oxford University Press, 1941